Pathways to Surrender

A Companion to Awakening

Michael Warmuth

and

Judy Flores

Also By The Authors

Opening and Allowing

DEDICATION

This book is dedicated to all those before us who consciously chose - and those after us who will consciously choose – to make surrender to Truth the main focus of their lives. Their commitment makes it easier for those who follow, and for this we are grateful.

CONTENTS

ACKNOWLEDGMENTS

Michael and Judy would like to acknowledge the tremendous amount of work put in by Sandy Callender and Janet Saunders in editing and reviewing the contents of this book. The way the material arrives means that it is not always easily converted to written word, and we are grateful for the skills and knowledge Sandy and Janet brought to this task.

We would also like to thank all of our friends, who have been so supportive and encouraging of our work to bring this book to the world.

INTRODUCTION

This book is a collection of guided meditations led by Michael, which were recorded and then transcribed by Judy. This process has been part of our morning meditations since 2011, and we have selected these particular meditations for you as a good sample of the topics that have been covered. They all have one thing in common – they describe in some way a journey to surrender. By surrender we mean the letting go of false ideas, beliefs and identity, and realization of our true nature. We see this as a universal approach to spiritual development, something that has been part of every true spiritual teaching since time began.

There is not necessarily any order to the meditations as far as subject or contents, they are arranged in the order they were delivered.

We wish you all the best in your journey and know that just the fact that you are reading this now means there is something here for you.

If you are not aware of the process in which Michael delivers these meditations, there is a short description at the end of the book. You can visit www.openingandallowing.com for more information and additional material. Our first book - Opening And Allowing - also gives the background to this whole process.

1. LET GO!

It is most important to remember that the spiritual universe operates on a quantum model as opposed to a Newtonian model. In other words, energy transforms instantly. Infinite possibilities exist all at once. In everyday language, miracles are normal. What is happening with you right now - the way your world looks and your body feels - is a direct result of what you imagine, dream, and create. Much of the time that imagining, dreaming, and creating is happening on a subconscious level - what you frequently end up with in your world is the product of your subconscious mind.

So we seek to become more conscious all the time - conscious of all the ways our body and mind are recreating the past for us and conscious of how to take control of our creative power with our conscious mind. By slipping into deep states of meditation, our conscious mind becomes the director of our creative power. By giving up and letting go of controlling the world, we allow life to become the spontaneous, joyful expression it's created to be. By surrendering, our limitations and resistance dissolve. We must remember to have compassion for ourselves and understand it is natural that our

1

subconscious mind should be so powerful in creating our lives. We also need to remember that we have free will to choose at any moment to let go and change can occur in an instant.

Miracles can happen at any moment. The world begins anew no matter what we have set in place; the world begins anew every moment. We are not victims of our subconscious mind. We are not victims of anything. We are evolving beings increasingly gaining control over our subconscious, spending more time living in a conscious way, gaining creative power, living more spontaneously, and loving more joyfully.

Life is cyclic in nature. We always dip into the past to undo and let go of subconscious limitations and return to the present, remembering the truth. Our task is not to eliminate our limitations completely, but to be conscious enough to love, accept and to have compassion for ourselves in every moment.

The truth is that we are sacred and divine beings. We are vulnerable. We are loving and loved expressions of one divine power. There is only divine love; it's what we are made of. It's what we are made out of. It's what we exist within. Every cell of our being radiates with God's love. Our heart beats by God's love. Our breath is breathed by God's love. Our mind is activated by God's love. It is not something we earn, become worthy of, or deserve. It is who we are and always have been whether we know it or not. God has held us in love since the beginning of time and always will. It is irrelevant whether or not we were conscious of love - whether we feel loved or not, or whether we feel worthy or adequate. All of that is irrelevant. In the eyes of God, we have been unfolding perfectly as the precious offspring of it's love. That love is alive right now. That divine radiance is bright. In truth, you are the divine radiance. You are not the body. You are not your thoughts. You are not your thinking mind. You are the light within. You are an infinite and eternal being, using this body and this mind to incarnate.

Activate feelings of compassion, understanding, love, gratitude to this body and mind. This body is your pathway to self-knowing, to self-reflection, and to experiencing. It's your mirror. It is not you. Evolution is a process of metamorphosis and transformation - bringing physical form to spiritual perfection. The pain and struggles were necessary. The challenges, the difficulties, the obstacles were all part of the divine natural order for your evolution – they were there for your soul to expand. Bring gratitude to your body for its service to you, for its years in the desert wandering lost. Bring love and compassion to yourself. Bring gratitude to the lost child that, despite all obstacles, continued on the path - despite uncertainty, despite not being sure of where to go or how to be. Something inside of that child continued to guide it and keep it on the path despite the pain, the struggle, and the confusion.

Now there is no question of who you are. Now there is no question that you are a beautiful child of God. Love is your divine birthright. Within you now is all the love possibility. Heal yourself in this moment. You are evolving, growing and expanding, letting go of limitations, fear, and confusion. Let it go. You now know you can surrender - you can let go. You know now that God is on your side and will perform miracles, send angels, and inspire you. Whether you forget again or not does not matter. You will always return to the truth. You are a conscious being. You are light. Nothing can change that now. Nothing can stop your evolution. Nothing can stop your expansion. Nothing can stop you from becoming the greatest expression of yourself. Your evolution is simply a matter of loving and letting go. The light and the love are strong within you. Right now - this moment - open your heart and your mind and let it fill your awareness. Let it go now. Feel yourself soften, melt, drift. Hold on to nothing. Trust God to guide you home. Trust God to support you and hold you - to love you. The loving eyes of God see beauty in you. Let go. Let go.

2. I AM NOT THAT

In order to achieve the kind of mind-set that goes along with manifesting healing and creating, one has to be able to activate a different mind, a different persona. It is not a persona; it is different from the normal persona or personality that drives most day-to-day thinking and behaving. It involves moving into a state of surrender at will, being able to distinguish immediately when one has slipped out of that state of surrender and moving back in simply by noticing the difference. This, of course, is an art and a skill that is practiced over and over again, particularly in meditation - always bringing one's attention back to the moment, back to the presence within.

Part of this new mindset is an acknowledgement and acceptance of the truth that everything is perfect, everything is evolving perfectly and there is no lack, illness, accident or mistake. It is a recognition that there are infinite possibilities in every moment. All this is the context for the creative, manifesting, prosperous, abundant mindset.

You can catch your thoughts and affirm the truth every time they are taking you in a different direction. You are training the mind to stay away from your ego's belief systems. So much of it is habit. Of course, beliefs must be changed on a subconscious level, but one has to change the context in which one is living. No matter what appearances look like or what your beliefs are in that moment, no matter what you feel like or look like, you have to act as if you believe the truth, as if you know the truth. For the truth is the truth; there is no question about it.

The ego is always trying to dominate, to control your mind space - to be the context. But you have the power to say, *No, that is not me. That is not who I am. That is not the truth and that is not reality.* This is how it works: you affirm the truth, you memorize the truth, you remember that within you, alive within you, is the presence of God. You remember you are not separate. It is impossible for you to be separate. It is impossible for you to be alone or unloved. Your ego may scream at you, argue with you, but you don't have to fight with it. Just observe it for what it is. It thinks it is doing it's best for you but you know better. There is a you that observes that ego. There is a you that can see, can decide, that there is another reality. This you is bigger than that ego - bigger than your subconscious mind. It is aligned with the one power. It is alive within you. It is always there, always ready, always available. But you must activate it. You must bring it into awareness. You must call it into being. Simply the act of stating *I am not that* activates a higher state of being, a higher context.

Continuing the process of stating what you are opens your context even further, giving you space to surrender and go to the truth. You can disempower the ego and open your mind to this spacious context that is alive in every moment. It's alive right now. It is available to you in every moment you choose to bring it forth. Now that you know the truth you can let go, you can trust God, you can surrender, you can remember the perfection in this moment. This bigger context is alive within you now: the spaciousness, the infinite, the eternal. And there is love here.

Allow your heart to open, to feel gratitude, love, thankfulness, for you are truly blessed and there is so much more to come. You know that. It is important for you to know that everything you are looking for exists within you right now. It is available to you right now. The only thing that stops you from experiencing it is your insistence that it isn't there. You know well enough now, you have heard it from so many teachers: everything you are looking for is there. When it seems that what you want or need is not there, acknowledge your insistence that it isn't. Make it as conscious as possible. Acknowledge your choice in that moment to insist that something is not there and then observe your reactions.

3. HEALING MEDITATION

To start with it is good to open the chakras and get into the energy of each chakra. Begin by placing all your attention on the 7th chakra. Become totally absorbed in that area at the top of your head; make it the focus of all your awareness. As you focus on it, feel the energy and become present as you direct all your awareness on that area. Let your body relax. Keep your mind focused. Now bring that awareness and that energy down to your 6th chakra between your eyes – the third eye - and feel the link between the 6th and 7th chakra. Go through the remaining chakras: 5th - throat, 4th - heart, 3rd - solar plexus, 2nd - abdomen, and 1st - tailbone, in like manner.

Healing is a process of returning to an absolute knowing and experience of love, truth, of the presence of God within you. To the degree that you are blocked from experiencing this, your healing will be affected. It is more difficult to know the truth in the midst of physical evidence of imperfection, of injury and illness. For these appearances tug at the ego and act as proof that there is something wrong. And so the ego gets reinforced and old patterns emerge - old habits of thought, old ways of being.

Surrender becomes difficult in the face of evidence and the grip of the ego, but it is not impossible. It is important to remember that injuries, illnesses, and accidents are a reflection of an energetic process. They are a physical out-picturing of a mental process. Healing is greatly assisted by understanding and letting go of whatever emotional process led to the breakdown in the first place. Sometimes it is not so apparent and is difficult to understand, but clarity will come if one is determined to retain an open mind and to attain true understanding.

If you want to heal a specific injury or illness, take a moment now and ask yourself, *What is this about? What did I need to learn that made this happen? How have I blocked energy that out-pictures this?* Take a moment now to ask yourself and let the answer come to you.

Once you have received an answer you are free to proceed with remembering the truth about yourself and to forgive yourself for needing to learn the lesson in such a hard way. Forgive yourself in this moment. It simply means letting go of any shame, blame or guilt, taking a compassionate approach toward yourself and knowing that it could not have been any other way. There is no place for and there are no regrets, no mistakes, and no accidents. Forgive yourself deeply and completely. Now is the time for you to become the loving parent to the child who has learned the hard way. It is time to open your heart, to feel the compassion for someone who has undergone such pain and, out of innocence, had no way to understand it. Open your heart.

Now it is time for you to know the truth, to be the truth, to be the presence of love, to be the one power, to be the surrendered and loving creator, to remember who you really are, to let go. Just let go. Let go now. Love is here. The light is alive within you. It's been here all along. It continues to bring healing to you even when you don't know it - even when you can't surrender to it. It continues to bring expansion and power into your life, even when you resist it. Let go now and let the light come. Say *yes* to it. Say *Yes, I am willing to open and let go in order to let my true nature shine through - to let the one presence within me come to life within me. I can and will surrender. I choose to let go. I choose to say yes. The healing power is alive within me. The loving restorative power of pure spirit restores everything to brand new. My body is created new in every moment and as I free my spirit I am made new.*

The loving presence is here now. Open yourself. Open your heart. Allow it to rise up in you.

4. ACTION

One of the greatest paradoxes of being human is that the desire or impulsion to act is always both an act of God and, in most cases, an act of the ego. This is one of the greatest dilemmas for individuals who are beginning to understand the nature of consciousness and their own true nature: they feel called to act, but are reminded to act only from inspiration. When one is acting from inspiration, the universe appears to conspire to make things line up to assist you, to put things in front of you that assist you and to put people in front of you that assist you. When you see this happening, you know you are truly acting from inspiration.

There are times when you don't seem to be able to accomplish anything and it feels like pain, resistance and torture and yet you feel compelled to act. Both actions are actions of God. How could this be? Is it necessary to feel compelled to do something when it is nothing but struggle? Is there a way to know at the outset whether or not one is on an inspired path?

There is an easy way to find out. Anytime you are engaged in action that feels like resistance and struggle or hard work....stop. Stop and pay attention to your level of surrender and connection to God. Do a thorough inventory of your internal presence and see how much resistance you have. If you are in the divine flow, you will have no resistance to stopping and connecting with God because God will be right there. If you are acting from ego, even the notion of stopping and connecting will feel like resistance and struggle, and you will know for certain you are not in the divine flow. This may seem rather obvious, but one of the true markers of an ego-compelled action is that you won't even remember to try to stop. Now that you have heard this, now that you know there is a way to know, you can change your consciousness.

How can both actions be acts of God? Because that's all there is. Even the ego is a creation of God. Because there is only one force and one power, nothing can be done without it. Does it mean that you are powerless to change the course of your life? No, it certainly does not mean that. You have the ability to make choices. You have the ability to know the truth or to believe the stories – you have the ability to surrender to your belief systems, to step down the evolutionary ladder. It is not a judgment or a criticism. It is not a question of value. It is a process by which you grow stronger, clearer, more conscious and able to choose. Remember that everything you experience, every single bit of struggle and pain and all the joy, is perfectly designed to bring you into a state of being a perfect expression of God as you are intended to be. You were never intended to be perfectly enlightened yesterday, the day before, or this morning.

There are challenges, obstacles to growth that had to happen. That very struggle has made you stronger and wiser. It is your choice whether to see them as true or to perceive it as a victim. But it is inevitable that you will see the truth of it and one day you will be grateful for all of it. You will understand how absolutely necessary it was. You will see the divine perfection in the whole journey. One day you will cry tears of joy for all you have experienced. One day you will be filled with a love so profound for those who seemed to have made your life so difficult. One day you will love yourself deeply and profoundly and you will recognize the beauty, splendor and perfection of you and your life. You will also realize that perfection is true right now.

You are not evolving into a perfect being; you are evolving into a being that recognizes their perfection. It is not that you have to improve yourself; you have only to improve your view of yourself. That is all that's necessary. You do not need fixing; you do not need repair. You are a pure, divine emanation of God. There cannot possibly be anything wrong with you. All you need to know is that you are perfect. It is a simple statement of truth.

This realization can happen in less than a moment. In an instant you can see the truth. There is nothing stopping you from knowing the truth except the nonsense that goes on in your mind: your identification with that lesser aspect of yourself, your insistence that you're not there yet, that you have something left to fix. You think you can't surrender yet: you don't know how, you are not good enough, and you're too scared.

All these thoughts are a thin veil. You're afraid of seeing the perfection, afraid of experiencing unconditional love, afraid of experiencing your divine nature, and afraid of surrendering control. The irony of controlling your life is that you are like a captain on a ship in a storm with no idea which way to go or how to get out of it. The master says, *I will guide you,* and will you say *no* for the shame of not having done it yourself? God will not take control of your ship if you do not want it. God will never force you to give up control. God can only love you and support you in every way possible, even when that way appears to be self-destructive, painful, or the wrong path. God will support you. There is no wrong path.

Do you understand how insignificant your resistance is to truth? Do you know how powerful truth is, how all pervading, how everything emerges from one Source, even your resistance? So, right now, in this moment you can let go and see it for what it is. You can get out of the way and let your vision be the true one. Let the presence and power of God within you be the focus of your awareness and let that truth be who you are. Identify yourself with God - the beauty, the joy, the creativity, and love.

Remember your birthright - your heritage is all the power in the world. It is unconditional love. It is alive in you right now. Don't cling to the wheel of a sinking ship. You know deep within your heart that God has never let you down. There is a place deep within you that knows you are loved unconditionally despite all the tragedy and trauma of your life - despite your firm conviction that God has let you down. There is nothing but God. There is no you that is not God. There is no separation. Bring all your awareness to the presence within you, the power that is alive within you, the elevated vibration that exists within you right now. Let go and surrender. Be still. Be quiet.

Now it's time to open your heart, to fill yourself with deep, loving gratitude for the recognition and realization that you are perfect, you are loved, and you chose to become the person you are becoming - a bigger expression of the one power than you have ever been before. You agreed and knew that you could conquer the challenges of your life in the interest of the greater expression of God in this time and place. You agreed. You said yes.

In recognition of your own courage, your own selflessness, allow yourself to feel love and gratitude. Rest in the knowledge that everything is perfect. Open your heart. From this place of loving acceptance direct your loving vision and loving energy to everything and everyone around you and see the perfection in everyone and everything. See the divine unfold as the perfect idea in the mind of God. Love and support that vision and see how you are called to be the love. You are the important one. It is your love, your unconditional loving acceptance, which makes the difference. It is you.

5. WE ARE GOD

The purpose of this meditation is to bring you back to the true
voice within you, the voice of truth. Our minds are
preoccupied with voices from the past, voices from our history,
belief systems, fear - the voice of control. We listen and argue
with it all day long and get nowhere. This voice is as clever as
we are; it always has an answer - it always has another reason
to keep listening to it. This voice protests, argues, creates fear,
has a hundred compelling reasons why we should pay
attention to it. It continues chattering to try to divert us. To
activate our fear, it sends signals to our nervous system to tell
us we are about to do something dangerous. We are beginning
to understand that we have a choice of whether we listen to
that voice or move to the voice of truth and shift our awareness
to a higher voice within us.

The mind and the brain are magnificent instruments. As soon
as we begin to focus our mind on something else, that voice
begins to dwindle, to lose its power. It's merely a collection of
neural pathways; it's nothing but electrical current going one
way instead of another. It has no reality. It's easy enough to
change that electrical current simply by focusing on something

else.

If we focus on something else our mind opens and we can remember that none of what happens in the *real* world has power nor is it real. Nothing in the material world has power. For even the electricity that fires in our mind and brain is the substance of God. Even the mindless chatter of our ego can happen only because God animates it. Even the struggle, the pain, the discomfort, and anything we experience is a product of God's power. Without God's power there is nothing. God's power animates our mind through a process of evolution and growth.

Our mind has developed a way of using energy to create a world we are comfortable with. Whether we like it or not, we choose what we are comfortable with - we choose the familiar. God's energy is used to create a familiar world for us until one day we wake up and realize that we are using little of what is available to us, so little of what we are capable of, so little of the amazing opportunities, possibilities, and infinite potential within us.

Generally our mind is stuck. Rarely do we have a new thought. We do everything by habit. We look for the old way of doing something instead of a new way. And yet, we are capable of doing almost anything. We are capable of magic, of miracles, of manifesting, of creating, of healing.

We are God. It may sound arrogant. It scares us to think of it. We can come up with a million reasons why we aren't God. How do we justify the life we live if we really are God? How do we justify our beliefs, our complaints, our history, our past? How are we going to live if we are God? What else could be the truth? What else could there possibly be? It is as Marianne

Williamson said, *It is not our weakness that we fear; it is our magnificence.* It is the power. It is the greatness.

Allow yourself to remember that there is nothing but God – absolutely nothing. Allow yourself to know that presence within you, to know that light within you. Just let yourself surrender. Let go. The old is giving way. You cannot use your old mind to bring you into your new life. Your old mind must give way. You have outgrown it. There is a new mind for you, a bigger one you have turned away from that has been there all along. You had other things to do first. Now it's time to return to the true nature of yourself.

The mighty loving power of God is upon you, calling you forth right here and now. There is nothing to fear, nothing to hold onto, and nothing to lose. Give your mind up to God. Open your mind; step out of the way. Let God fill you with the divine spirit - with its love, its joy, its beauty. You are called to a greater destiny. You are called by a mighty power to be a shining example of the power of love in your life, to surrender your will to God, to give up the fight, give up the struggle, give up the resistance. Your journey through the dark forest is over. The castle of riches is in front of you. It is yours.

Open your heart now. Your heart is the gateway to the castle, to the riches, to the full expression of your divine purpose. Allow your heart to open. Allow love to be your truth. Don't be afraid to open your heart. You are safe. There is a gentle, loving presence here for you - a warm, loving presence inside you and around you. You are in a sea of love. Every cell of your being is energized with the power of love, vibrating with the power of love. Your body is made of love. Your thoughts are powered by love. Your breath is energized by love. Your heart beats by the electricity of love.

Let your heart open. God is here right now in this moment, in this place. The power of God is alive within you. Let go of everything; let it all go. Let go of everything. Let the light and power of God's loving flame within you dissolve everything. There is nothing that you need but the power of God. Everything you need is contained within that light within you – everything: all knowledge, all wisdom, all power, all creativity, all joy. It's already in you. Don't hold onto anything. Let it go. Let yourself become a blank slate for God. Let God be you. You don't need your old way of being anymore.

6. RAISING YOUR VIBRATION

Whatever you may be experiencing right now, whatever you have chosen to pay attention to, whatever is demanding your attention, there remains a truth that is unchanging, unchangeable, infinite and eternal and always present within you. At times this seems impossible to believe, impossible to connect with, impossible to understand or that it could be true in this moment, but it is.

When you are not paying attention to the infinite within you, you are engaged in a never-ending cycle of control, stress, resistance, powerlessness, and victimhood. Once this cycle captivates your awareness, it gains strength and grows stronger. It has the ability to cause you pain, to capture your thinking, and to keep you distracted.

In the normal course of events we don't make the effort to return to the truth until it is too uncomfortable to do anything else. By then it is much more difficult. Old cycles of trauma are activated, old beliefs are in full strength, old defenses and resistance structures are full of power until we reach the point where we can take it no longer and decide we must get back to surrender. It seems like a tiresome way to live, but in actuality no one has ever lived any differently.

The truth is that the more you surrender, the more you let go, the sooner you become uncomfortable with *not* being surrendered. Surrendering raises your vibration - raising your set point. You begin to have less and less tolerance for discomfort - for being un-surrendered. You begin to recognize the symptoms of resistance right away. And all the while, in every moment, the truth is alive within you, the presence of God is alive within you, all the power to heal, manifest, and create is within you ready to be used. All the while a powerful new way of being is already active within you, waiting for you to allow it to express itself.

You do not have to create your new being from scratch. You don't have to do hard work to build a new personality. You don't have to come up with some new idea. It's already alive in you. It's already there. You just have to let it out. You don't have to know anything except how to let go, how to surrender, how to know that it's time to let go. You just have to remember. That is your only task.

The mind and power of God - infinite wisdom - already has it taken care of. There are no parts of the puzzle missing; there is nothing wrong. Everything already exists perfectly. Are you willing to let that be the truth of your life? Are you willing to hand over control? Are you willing to surrender your will, your determination to do it your way, your desire to take care of yourself? Are you willing to let go of that? Are you willing to believe and trust that there is a power within you that already knows how to make sure that all your needs are met, a power that already knows how to heal anything that comes before you, a power that knows how to express itself perfectly, a power that is simply waiting for you to say *yes* to being it's vessel? Will you stop caring about how you look, about whether you are doing everything right, about whether you are good enough?

Just stop worrying and noticing everything you do wrong. Just stop measuring your shortcomings. Give up trying to fix your human mind with your human ideas. It can't be done. It's impossible. It's either true or it's not, and you know that it's true. You know deep in your heart there is only one God, only one power, and that power is the power for good. That power is infinite, eternal, and unconditionally loving. The only reason it doesn't have full expression in your life is because you won't let it. You won't trust it. You won't say *yes*. You won't give up control. You won't surrender. We know that the truth is that you are doing all that you can to surrender, to trust, to let go, to say *yes.*

We highlight the resistance to make it palpable, to make it clear, to make it stand out in your mind so it is obvious that the only thing that stops you from having everything you need and want is your own resistance. This is not to judge you or blame you or make you feel guilty or responsible. It's just to encourage you to let go a little bit more. Just say *yes* a little bit more. Do that now. Let go.

7. SURRENDER

As products of our society, culture and families, it's hard for us to accept and understand that there is really nothing for us to do. Those who of us who have experienced a lot of trauma have shut down and closed off the alive and spontaneous parts of ourselves. We have had to do everything by exerting our will. Everything has taken effort. Even the things we enjoy have often taken effort. Just moving our body has required the use of will. We have been so accustomed to this way of being that we don't understand that our bodies, our minds, our very beings are completely capable of spontaneous action, spontaneous creativity, spontaneous thought. It requires no effort, no will. It only requires surrender.

So now, when we understand how we have limited ourselves and are beginning to see the big picture of how many possibilities and opportunities we have, there is a part of us that still completely rejects and is terrified by this whole process. We fear having to engage our will again and again, having to do things just to look good and look as if we are engaged until we are exhausted from it all. We think we have to look right, to do it right, to have to meet some standard. We forget that this is the old way. We're trying to understand how to be free from the perspective of being in jail. It can't be done. We are truly free only when we are unable to stop ourselves. The truth is that what actually leaves us worn out, stressed out, tired of the same old thing, is the large amount of energy that it takes to stop ourselves from being creative, spontaneous, alive, peaceful. That is what consumes all of our energy and then, on top of that, we feel we have to use our will to accomplish anything.

That is not the way we are designed. That is not the idea in the mind of God. Who we are, what we are, how we are, is an idea that originates in the mind of God, and is expressed through our mind. There is an ever-flowing energetic expression that creates our life. We tire ourselves out trying to contain it, trying to block it, hide it, and control it. The irony of all of this is that there is nothing for us to do. God will do it all if we will only let go. Instead, we feel that we can't face the prospect of dragging ourselves up another notch and forcing ourselves into a higher vibration. We don't realize that we are better off doing nothing rather than forcing ourselves or using our will. We cannot let fears that arise from living cause us to lose the path and wobble on our commitment to become all that our lives are meant to be. All we will get is more of the same until we choose to stay surrendered, until we make staying surrendered our goal in every minute of the day.

What we are so afraid of is already true about us. It's been true about us since the beginning of time; we have only convinced ourselves to not to believe that we are one with God. This is nonsense. We cannot change ourselves into something less than God. All our belief systems and all our stories from our past are elaborate illusions that have nothing to do with truth. Right now the light shines brightly in every one of us. Every one of us has our full potential at hand. Every one of us has infinite possibilities and opportunities every moment. Our evolution is already complete in the world of truth. In truth there is no time or space. There is no imperfection, there is no lack, no sickness; there is no pain or struggle. All of that is true right now in every one of us.

The fact that you may choose to believe otherwise right now has no impact on the truth. The fact that you may not be able to experience that truth has no impact on it. It doesn't make it any less true. The feeble arguments have no impact on it. There is nothing we can do to cause lack in God. There is nothing we can do to cause illness in God. There is nothing we can do to cause imperfection. But we can choose to stop arguing against it; we can choose surrender.

There is great fear around surrender. Why is that? We are afraid we will disappear, afraid we will cease to exist, which often has us feeling as if we might die. The biggest fear is that we will cease to exist, that there will be no place where we are. Now, you know who is doing the thinking: it is not the mind of God. The mind of God energizes those thoughts. The ego that thinks such thoughts is indeed a creation of God but it's not God. That's not who you are. The ego is a physical process - an effect, not a cause.

Our thoughts are just part of the body trying to stay alive. They are not cause in this world in the way that God is. Our unconscious belief systems shape creation, but they are not the source of creation. That is who you truly are: you are not shaping creation, you are the source of creation - you are one with God, right here right now. The presence of God is alive within you waiting for you to step out of the way. Stop fighting, arguing, and resisting. Choose to let go now.

Surrender to the presence within you. Choose to trust. There's a bigger, more loving, more powerful being inside you that is untouched by the thoughts and fears - it is great, infinite, eternal, ever expanding. Your very existence is totally an idea in the mind of God. This physical form is merely the after-effect of something that has already happened. You can let go; you can surrender. Your mind can rest. This power, this presence, this spirit that moves you, reminds you of who you are. As your heart opens, there are parts of your being you have been afraid of, ashamed of, and you have not wanted to be conscious of. Repressing these aspects of you keeps you in pain and struggle - keeps you from being totally surrendered. It is important that you bring love - bring the consciousness of divine spirit - into every aspect of your being so that you can know your own true wholeness and perfection. Get out of the way and let the love and the light fill you up. Every cell of your being vibrates with the love of God.

8. PAIN, STRUGGLE, HEALING

It is tempting to believe in the power of the physical world and the reality of pain, imperfection, lack, and the inadequacy of ourselves when we are presented with the overwhelming evidence of our imperfection. We can easily believe that somehow we are falling short; somehow we are not getting it - that we're not good enough. It will always be this way when we look through the world of form for answers or solutions or relief. It is so important to remember that your physical expression is a nebulous and temporary phenomenon; it is not a real thing. It is not permanent, not cast in stone, or on a pathway that is circumscribed by the past history. It is something that can change in a moment. It can heal in an instant; it can let go in any moment. This does not mean to say that we should not continue to endeavor to work with our bodies; it takes a very high degree of spiritual development to change your body on a moment-to-moment basis.

It takes a high degree of surrender to miracles to be able to ignore symptoms, tension, and the resistance. But you can always remember the truth and not get caught in the stories, the pain and resistance. It is easy to believe the stories, and to believe that they have power - that they are setting your destiny. But you can return to the higher perspective, the higher view. You can remember that within you is perfection: a perfect spirit, a perfect God, a perfect power. You can remember that all of your pain and struggle is releasing your barriers to knowing your truest self. When your body is fighting against surrendering, against opening to love and experiencing vulnerability and hurt, pain is experienced because your body knows no better. In that way it is programmed to survive - and it has.

But there is another part of you that knows what is missing. It remembers joy, freedom, ecstasy, and love. That part of you is always trying to move back to that experience to recover your birthright. But it doesn't feel safe. It doesn't trust. It has been hurt too many times. There is only one power to solve this problem; there is only one true solution. There is only one truth about who you are. When you are engaged in the battle of resistance you cannot remember this truth - you cannot know it but it is still true. It seems impossible to believe that within you in every moment is all the love, all the peace, all the power that you can imagine. It is all there alive within you. All the acceptance of you just as you are, all the unconditional love for you just as you are, all the compassion and understanding just as you are. It exists within you right now.

You can surrender to this power. This is an extremely frightening idea: to really open, to let go of control, to hand your life over. It seems more frightening than living with pain. What you need now is a compassionate, loving, healing power. Allow that energy to move through you. Allow the cells of your body to experience that loving, accepting, understanding, unconditional compassion, the love of Jesus, the gurus, the mystics - the powerful presence of love. Allow yourself to be healed. Let the powerful, loving presence soothe you, hold you, and protect you. Let your resistance dissolve and know that you are precious. You are precious – it is true. You are a miracle; you are one with God. You are wanted. There is a loving light in you that has always been there - will always be there. There is an eternal and infinite presence, a perfect loving presence that wants only the best for you, that wants you to know the truth of who you are, to know how important you are, how loved you are. Pay attention to that love. Pay attention to that presence. It is alive within you. Let it grow in you. Let it expand to fill your mind.

Pay attention to it. It wants to heal you. It wants to make you whole. It wants to bring you love. Everything you need is within you.....everything. It's time to choose, to surrender, to say yes to love, to say yes to God. You are safe now. There is no danger. No harm will come to you. You can let go. You can trust.

9. INNER CHILD

When your body is reacting and there doesn't seem to be any
way to achieve peace to get back to connection and surrender,
you become a victim and slip into an old habit of trying to
control your body - trying to fix it - believing there is
something wrong. What is actually happening is that your
higher self, your observer, has abdicated, and you have moved
into a state of polarization where there is good and bad, right
and wrong, and not enough – a place where the physical world
is the primary reality and where what is happening in the
physical world really does matter and is more important than
what is happening in your mind. The cycle of events has been
triggered and very powerful survival chemicals have been
released into your system. Your body is in a full survival
reaction. It seems that there is no way out.

This is when it is most difficult to establish the truth in your
thoughts, to connect with that higher self that knows the truth,
and can observe dispassionately the body's and the mind's
attempt to work things out in the physical world. And this is
exactly what is required. There is much resistance to opening
to the higher truth from the ego and the body. There is a fear
of being overpowered. This is the replay of old trauma. This is
the replay of an overpowered, overwhelmed child with

nowhere to go for safety, no one to rely on, nothing to trust in except one's physical resources. There is no God available or so it seems. But that is no longer true.

There is an adult present within you. That adult had very poor training in how to deal with an overwhelmed child, so it adopted the way of the adults it was surrounded by which simply continues the trauma. That adult now begins to acknowledge and accept the pain and the overwhelming fears of that child - begins to let that experience permeate so that the adult brings compassion, understanding, love, and comfort to the child. That adult becomes someone trustworthy for the child to reach out to. That adult reaches out to the child and recognizes the confusion.

This is the time to pray. In the beginning there may be no sense of achieving any connection with God or of achieving any sense of relief. But there must be a remembering and acknowledging of the truth, a reaching out to the child who has developed much fear of reaching out to a God who doesn't seem to be there. The more the adult acknowledges the pain and opens to the distress and confusion, the more the child will be able to reach out. There has been a very hard line between the child and the adult, a firm barrier. The adult, believing it was the authentic identity, banished the child, preventing the discomfort and confusion.

The child is life. The child is creativity and innocence. The child is the power of the light and love. The child contains the seed of everything. The child does not condemn or judge. It seeks only freedom - the right to be, to express, to be joyful, happy, loving, playful, creative, trusting. Here is the opportunity to acknowledge that true identity, the true self, which is not a controlling parent. The control was merely a survival tool rendered obsolete as soon as you were independent. The real you is ready to be born again, to forgive and forget and start from this moment.

Become the child right now. Become the light. Become the forgiving, innocent, loving presence. You are not judged. You are not wrong. You are not bad. You are not alone. You are as perfect and beautiful as you were in the mind of God in the very beginning. You are alive. You are well. You have done your job. You have protected that precious light within you in the only way you knew how. In the most extreme of circumstances you kept that light alive and it still is alive and it loves you for what you have done. It is understanding, it acknowledges the difficulty, the sacrifices you have made and wants you to know that it will all be made up to you in ways you can't even imagine.

You are a beautiful soul, you are a special being, and you have accomplished a difficult task. There is no judgment; there is only recognition of a beautiful being of light. Now you no longer have to fear the judgment of God or anyone else. The love is in you. God is in you and always has been and always will. Just let it in.

Grief is healing; it brings you back to life. Do not question, doubt, or analyze it. It is life returning. It is the power of love restoring you to openness and oneness - to wholeness. It is the cracking of the ice. The grief is your soul breaking through to the essence of God within you. Be grateful. Be glad. You are alive, you are loved, and you can love. You are not alone; you are not separate. You are significant and important; you are precious and beautiful. You are a perfect expression of the one power.

10. MIRACLES

Today is a good day to expect miracles. At any moment you can change your mind and expect miracles. Why do you look for what is wrong with the day and not just expect another day of miracles? How hard would it be to change your mind? How hard could it be to remind yourself that in every moment miracles abound around you, that possibilities endlessly abound? Did you forget the truth? Here is a secret: remind yourself at any given moment about the truth, the possibility of miracles, about the infinite possibilities, about the one power. Just reminding yourself in that moment will do more for you than you can imagine.

Is it possible that we choose a more comfortable approach instead of choosing possibility - of choosing miracles, of loving ourselves, of remembering our own perfection? It seems like too much trouble. It doesn't seem possible and we think we are much more comfortable limping along hoping we will be enlightened one day, hoping we will learn to surrender. We have many, many years of practicing that way of thinking. We have generations of conditioning and support for that comfortable way of thinking.

Keep your mind on miracles. Look for them everywhere; see them happening all around you. Understand what a miracle your life is. Acknowledge that. Spend your time on that. The physics of your life is so improbable. No mathematician would ever bet on it. The odds against you turning up like this are as close to impossible as you can get. This life, this physical being is the result of an incredible mind, and it's all powered by love. Love is the basis of every aspect of you.

What is amazing about our lives is not that we find love, but that we don't even though that's all there is. We are so powerful, we are so clever, we are so imaginative that we can even make ourselves feel bad when we live in love, are surrounded by it, filled with it, and made from it. If we should ever doubt that we are powerful, creative beings, we only need to understand how powerfully we have worked to shut out our own light and power, a power that is vast beyond imagining. We need feel no shame or guilt; there is no judgment. We only need to stand in awe at the power of our own minds. We have the supreme intelligence of the one source backing us up whatever way we want - creating and manifesting instantly.

And so we turn our minds now to remembering the truth: that there is only one source, one power, one God. We know this to be true; it is built into our very fabric. We know that it is impossible for it to be any other way. We know that at one time in our life we trusted God; we lived in bliss and peace. That memory is encoded in us whether we can access it consciously or not. There is a knowing in us that we are a child of God, that the world is a beautiful place, that there is peace and love and abundance and all our needs are met, that there is joy, creativity, fun, miracles. We know this. When we hear it we know it is true. When someone speaks it, it resonates deep within us. We cannot deny it. The spirit in us calls to the spirit

34

in another. We are being called deeper into our true nature. We are called to shatter the mask, to stop pretending that we are somehow ineffective, defective, unworthy. We are being called to remove the hood from the light within us that we have so zealously kept in place.

We know that we can surrender to the presence within us. We can quiet our mind, let go of the fear, choose to return to the truth. Do that now. Choose. Say in this moment, *I choose to surrender to the presence within me. I choose to focus on the truth that there is only love. I do not need my ego to protect me from God. I choose to let go right now.*

11. JUST ALLOW

In this meditation our goal is to move into a state of consciousness that allows and accepts the truth of our being as one with God. In this state we are willing to surrender our will and trust in God's divine idea for us. It is a state of knowing that all of our needs are met, that we are healthy, loved and loving, that we are made in the image and likeness of God, and that we are indeed inseparable from God and one in the mind of God. This is always true whether we are aware of it or not; our awareness has no impact on it whatsoever. It is still always the truth.

But in our day-to-day lives we are not truly present - not presents in our bodies, not present in our thoughts, not present in directing the focus of our awareness. We let our awareness be captured constantly by the distractions of our mind and body and the outside world. The longer we allow that to go on, the further and further we get from the truth, until we remember to remind ourselves to get present. So that is our goal in this moment: to become truly present, to withdraw our awareness and attention from our thoughts and other distractions and just become aware of this moment.

In this moment there is an energy, a potential. There is life, power, and possibility in this moment. Allow yourself to let go of control, to let go of fear, to let go of having to do anything. Just stop. Stop trying. Just pay attention to what happens when you don't do anything, when you make no effort, when you let go of all trying, when you let go of all judgment, all condemnation, all analysis, all measurement, all comparison. There's no need for any of that. Whatever *is*, is. Just let whatever *is* be what it is. Just allow.

Your body is accomplishing a mind-boggling amount of tasks without any effort on your part. The city you live in is functioning just fine without any effort on your part. The earth is moving through space without any of your effort. There is nothing you can do to contribute any more. It is all happening perfectly in divine order without any effort on your part. Just get out of the way. Within you, your heart and soul are ready to express even more of who you are if you will just allow it to. The energy of spirit is waiting for you to get out of the way - to bring you peace, to bring you love, to express the divine attributes of God through you. You don't have to do anything; God knows how to do everything. Just get out of the way.

Why do you think you have to figure it out? You think you are smarter than God, that God doesn't know how to create a perfect life, that somehow God needs your help? God does need your help but not in the way you think. God needs you to allow its expression through your physical form. That means saying, *yes.* That means allowing. That means getting out of the way. You can make that choice right now. You can choose to open, to surrender, to allow. The power of God is alive within you. The presence is burning brightly within you. Let it grow. Let it be strong. Surrender to it. Let it fill you. There is no question that you are a perfect expression of the mind of God - that you exist only within the mind of God, that there is no part of you that exists outside of the mind of God. There is no question that there is only perfection in the mind of God. There are no mistakes. There's no question that you can transform your awareness in this moment. Open your heart to a feeling of deep gratitude for the precious gift that you have been given - your life.

12. TRAUMA

When something in the present triggers old trauma, our body goes into survival mode, releasing hormones, activating old reaction patterns, creating chaos and incoherence in our mind until we get to the point where we are completely locked into an old story, an old belief, an old way of being.

With our brain energized in this way, it is very difficult to gain clarity and remember the truth. In these situations a part of us has been activated that we don't want to know about, a part we want to disown. It doesn't fit with our idea of how we should be or who we should be; there is incongruence. Our immediate goal in the present moment is to make it go away again. But what is being activated is an authentic part of us - our life force seeking to be integrated again. And the part of us that is trying to make it go away is the old personality that we took on so that we could fit in and look good in whatever way we imagined that to be. In many ways we are acting as our own parent against our own child. We fear these hidden aspects of ourselves. We see them as a threat to our survival, so we think that all they are is a natural reaction to overwhelming and overpowering circumstances. On the contrary, these hidden aspects are our spirit, our life force in action. They are never anything bad or evil.

Our natural inclination is towards connection, loving, being part of a community. But because we chose to grow up in community and function in a whole and integrated way, we adapted ourselves to fit in - which meant suppressing our natural responses, stifling our natural desire to act with integrity, be authentic and expressive, and to speak the truth. So there is this part of us we must welcome back. We must use our ability to choose and to discern, to remember the truth, to choose the truth.

Our mind, our ego, has us totally convinced that there is no way out. We have become identified with victimhood and yet that is never our true identity. We always have a choice. We don't want to choose the truth because it means acknowledging that cut-off part of us, welcoming it back in, and acknowledging our own failure to be loving. We can choose the way of compassion, acceptance, and understanding. We can come back to the present, breathe, relax, and step back from the drama, step back from the dream world where things are good or bad, people are good or bad, we are good or bad. We can step back from that and remember the truth that no one has power over us. There is no one outside of us. There is only God. There is only love. Everything else is an illusion.

Our opportunity here is to become the expression of unconditional love, and that means loving ourselves. It is not about being a saint or a good person; it is about truly, deeply, being an expression of God, and then getting out of the way. This is not a job for the ego. This is not something that can be forced or acted. This is not about looking good. This is simply letting the truth be. In this moment - in every moment - the presence of God is alive within you, infinite and eternal, right now. Whether you feel it or not, whether you choose it or not, all of your existence right now is an expression of the love of God. Choose the higher path. Choose compassion. Choose love, forgiveness, acceptance. Choose to accept the truth. Don't fight it. Accept the presence of God within you. Say *yes* to it and don't push it away. Don't hold onto your resistance. Don't cling to your story. Let it all go. It's not taking you anywhere.

13. PAIN

Authors Note: It is important to understand the meaning of pain as it is used in this meditation. We asked for clarification and the answer we received essentially defined pain as the psychological response to a sensation in the body. The example was given of standing on something sharp. An immediate sensation is experienced, notification that we need to do something about what just happened. After that, our psychology takes over, and this is when pain becomes a factor. If we have feelings of resistance, of victimization, of being unfairly treated, we will experience pain. In this writing then, pain is not the sensation of some action needed, it is the psychological pain being discussed.

The presence of physical pain is always an indicator of resistance or holding - of clinging to an old pattern. Intense physical pain signifies a significant barrier - a significant amount of resistance to a new opening. It is easy to believe that something is terribly wrong and that somehow you are being punished - that there is some way in which this could have been avoided. The truth is that significant growth is always accompanied by significant pain.

It has become one of humanity's greatest priorities to eliminate pain, to avoid it, to anesthetize it. Yet when one looks at the very nature of transformation, it always includes pain. Humans and even other forms of life rarely feel the urge to take transformational steps if not motivated by pain. Pain is the messenger that the higher self is waiting; that a new self is waiting and ready to be born and something has to be released for this new self to emerge.

There are so many metaphors and analogies in nature for this transformational process. Human birth is a significant one. There is often much pain and struggle involved in the birthing process for the child as it emerges into the light and air, and for the woman as she is transformed into a mother. As always, it is easy to see yourself as a failure or to judge yourself for experiencing pain. The question of how you could have been better or how you could have done it differently, or what you missed, is a distraction to the simple questions: *What am I being called to let go of? How have I been limiting myself? Who am I being called to be now?*

In times of intense physical pain it is very difficult to remember that the physical world is just an out-picturing of your own consciousness. The pain you are experiencing is a block in the flow of energy. It is energy condensed until it is almost unmoving, relative to the true vibrational frequency of your true self. The answer does not lie in trying to fix the problem on the physical plane. That is the realm of secondary cause.

At some point you must simply give up and allow your own divine nature to take care of things in its own perfect way, in its own divine wisdom, its own supreme intelligence, its own complete perfection. It is not in your body that you have a problem. It is the filters you have added to your own perception of yourself and who you are, the limits you have placed on yourself, the way you stop yourself from expressing authentically, the way you limit your own unique and beautiful expression of God. It will be painful, especially if you don't take the time to learn the message the pain is giving you. As Abraham says, *don't worry it will just get louder.*

So we come back to remembering the truth: to knowing that we are connected to God, we are not alone and isolated, that despite what our mind or body is telling us, the truth of our own divine heritage cannot be denied. Any sense of separation is an illusion. Any belief of unworthiness is an illusion. Any idea whatsoever that we are anything less than God is a complete misconception, a mere activity of our mind trying to prevent us from taking a risk and letting go of control. There is nothing that needs to be fixed. There is nothing about our true nature that can be harmed, limited or denied in any way.

The presence of God is alive within us. We are alive within the presence of God. This higher vibration of light and beauty is the only true being. We have the power to imagine ourselves as something less or different but it is only our imagination.

We also have the ability to choose what we are aware of in this moment. We can choose to be aware of the presence of God within us, to be aware of the vibration and frequency of love as the very activity of our body. The very nature of our physical being is the vibration of love. We can choose to surrender, to let go, give up, to accept the mind of God. We can choose to allow it, to say *yes,* to get out of the way of our own divine nature, to stop covering it, hiding it, and stop trying to make it fit. Make the choice now. Choose to let God, your own divine nature flow through you. Allow yourself to get out of the way, to let go and experience the divinity within you.

14. THE CHILD

Imagine that somewhere there is a child who has grown up in
wonder, love, peace, joy, and creativity. She's still young, still
free; she has absolute faith and trust in the world. She has no
fear of the future, no trouble from the past; she has only the
moment to enjoy. She can't help singing and skipping and
dancing, smiling and laughing. She loves everyone she meets.
Dogs love her, cats love her; animals are not afraid of her and
she is not afraid of them. Often when she sees things she
doesn't like she just wishes them to be different and they are.
She doesn't even think about it because it always happens. Her
capacity to love is not fettered in any way. Her capacity to be
in wonder and awe is unlimited. She can't help making
everything fun. When people around her suffer she has the
ability to remind them of their own childlike nature. People
can't hang onto their victim stories because she sees right
through them. Her innocence about pain is authentic and
genuine. She does not threaten or challenge people; she just
loves them.

This is who you are. This is who lives within you. You are

innocent. You are pure. You are loving. You are creative and joyful and free. All of those qualities are in you. They are your nature. You know this to be true. But there is nothing easy about letting go of the old identity. We cling to our beliefs about ourselves. We insist that we are not innocent, pure, and free. We can cite all kinds of evidence that we are not free. Yet it is impossible for us not to be free, since nothing - absolutely nothing - restrains us except ourselves. As we awaken we begin to understand how it is that we set limits and create barriers that hold back love. We are our own worst enemy. Right here and right now, the state of perfection lives within you; the manifestation of God in time is expressing through you in this very moment. You are bringing God into this world. Let go now; let go of the ties, the chains, the knots. Let go of the need to control, the need to manage how you look, how you appear.

15. PERFECTION

You can neither please nor displease God. You must be constantly aware of who or what you think God is. God is not an entity, a being with thoughts and desires or feelings; you can't hurt God's feelings. God is a power, a presence. God is an intelligence. God does not care if you forget who you are. God is not offended and God does not punish you for doing things that don't seem in your best interest or in others. God can only do one thing: just *be* God. It is nearly impossible for our minds to conceive of eternity and infinity with no time and space, infinite intelligence, and perfect unconditional love. But those are the qualities of God. We, on the other hand, experience duality – good and bad, cold and hot, strong and weak, happy and sad, right and wrong. To our human mind it seems impossible that God could be separate from the world of duality. But it is true. God does not experience duality except through us.

We experience duality. Our bodies are the expression of duality, of yes and no, on and off, good and bad, right and wrong. They are the boundary between infinite and eternal and time and space. It is through our bodies that we experience both God and not God. Although there is truly no such thing as not-God, in our own mind we create feelings, thoughts, beliefs, and duality. We have yet to perfect the art of being non-dual in our bodies. To be non-dual is our dream, our deepest desire, our soul's longing. To experience perfection is what our body is for - so we can actually feel it and look in the mirror and see perfection in form – so we can hear it, feel it, taste it, experience it.

And here is the key: experience the perfection - it's happening all the time. There never is duality. There never is right or wrong, good or bad. All that is a story, an illusion. Even pain is perfect. If only we would stop judging, stop making things good or bad, right or wrong, or less than perfect. If only we would allow ourselves just to experience the perfection of what God has created. For some reason we believe that we must improve God's work. It's like giving a delicate and beautiful painting to a child to finish with crayons when the masterpiece is already here!

There is nothing you can do to improve on what God has created. It does not mean there are not things to do. Rather, the things to do are God's things, not yours. You are an illusion; you don't exist in the way you think you do. You don't exist as some sort of being here to test, here to struggle, here by yourself to figure things out. You think you are your body. You think you *are*. But in truth, any thought you think that contains any notion of imperfection is illusion. You think you are powerless to change things in your life. It's true that your illusory self is completely powerless. But your true self is capable of anything. Believing that you are your body - that you are of this world - is like believing that you are the bed you sleep in or the chair you sit in.

Right here and right now, the timeless, the eternal, the infinite is alive within you. In this moment there is only one truth. Why do you fight? You are afraid. You believe that you must be in charge - you must be in control. You believe that there is something to be afraid of - that you will truly lose your mind. You believe you have something to lose, that somehow you are better off holding on. Your ego says it knows the truth. Your ego says it knows what is best for you, and that it will keep you safe. It is a strange kind of safety compared with the loving peace that is your true nature - the unconditional love that lives within you, the infinite abundance, joy, creativity and power that is your true being. Let go. Don't fight. Choose to say yes. Choose to open. There is nothing awful inside you. There is nothing in you that will not heal. Let go. Surrender.

16. BELIEVING EGO

It's hard to imagine that a person would deliberately choose to think and feel in a way that makes them feel badly. It is hard to think that people would want to focus on a small slice of who they are and see that as the totality of their being. It is difficult to understand why someone would consciously refuse to acknowledge the truth of their being – that people would deny the feelings of love within them, that they would block creativity, throttle abundance, and stifle the joy. And yet, this is what the ego does. The ego says *no* to all of that, not in a way that could be described as conscious, but yet it is very deliberate.

When we are experiencing life from a narrow and limited view, we have put the ego in charge. When we have abandoned the truth and have submitted to the power and pressure of the ego, we do so out of habit or fear. It's amazing how quickly it happens. Just one little slip and the ego says, *See, I told you life isn't safe*, and the judgment begins. It's hard to believe that we would have any interest in going along with that at all when what's available to us is so much more fun, enjoyable, fulfilling, and rewarding. We continually deny our ability to access God: we say we can't have it, we don't know how, we're not there yet, it only happens to other people. But in truth, it's alive within us right now – right in this moment. There is nothing but goodness within us, nothing but love, nothing but one creative power.

No matter how we shape our arguments, they are futile. And why would we want to argue? Why wouldn't we just say *yes* to our own perfection? It's incredible the length of our list of rationalizations; it's awe-inspiring to see all of that creative power turned to justifying our own small view of ourselves. We even believe that there is goodness in being small - we believe that somehow we are more spiritual as we embrace our small self – we believe we have developed a greater sense of humility. We make a virtue of being poor - as if God has any view. As if somehow we can make ourselves better because God didn't make us good enough. As if we can improve from what we perceive to be God's faulty creation.

How do we continue to believe that somehow we know better than God? How is it that we imagine we are somehow a better judge? That we know more about right and wrong, good and bad? God does not have an agenda; God is just being God. That's all God can do. We have the amazing ability to recognize that we are God, and yet what we choose to recognize is that we are anything but; we are more interested in our imperfection than our perfection. We are obsessed with it. We tinker with it. We judge ourselves constantly. We rationalize, and justify.

But nobody's listening to us, except us. God is not listening - not to that. God is or God isn't. We are God or we aren't. We are perfect or we aren't. Our life is unfolding perfectly or it isn't. We are exactly where we should be or we aren't. We can make either one of them true, and they will be, but only to us. God is not a serious taskmaster who wants us to work hard at being good. God is a child who wants us to come out and play. God has no need for self-improvement or virtue. All we have to do is to let go. There are no rules. Every one of us is completely and totally unique. There cannot be any rules. We can't say that we trust God and rely on rules to protect us. We can't say that there is God and then not trust it.

The presence of God is alive within you right now, right here. The powerful, loving, creative power is alive within you right now. You are a conduit of this loving source. You are the gateway between the invisible and the visible. You are magnificent beyond belief. You have potential that is infinite; it is inconceivably vast. Love is your divine birthright, the substance in which you are made. It is what gives you life. It is what gives you the self-recognition. It is the only real power there is. Nothing lives without love. Nothing is created without the loving force of love. Every cell of your being vibrates with love. Give in to it. Surrender to it. Lay your ego down and let it go. Get out of your own way. Allow it to grow within you.

17. YOUR BIRTHRIGHT

We must start by remembering that surrender and letting go are conscious choices. They are decisions we make, intentions that we have. We are always reminding ourselves as our attention drifts that our intention is to surrender and let go in this moment. We remember and acknowledge that there is something sacred and holy within us. There is something sacred about the process of meditation and prayer. We use the power of our mind and intention to prepare ourselves to open and allow, to let go, to trust, to give in.

Until we are masters who live in the present most of the time, our mind and our body will attempt to distract us. So we must prepare our mind and body by remembering the truth and affirming it and making the choice to let go and say *yes* to surrendering knowing that there is within us in this moment the light and presence of God. Focusing on the present moment and relaxing into our bodies we make the decision to let go, to give up. We begin to become aware of an expanded energy within us. We don't try to control; we just let go. We move into the present.

It is not unusual to run into fear when we let go and surrender. We remind ourselves that fear is obsolete; it has no relevance. Our survival mechanisms are of no use to us in this realm. There is nothing to fear. We are not in danger. We are not going to be annihilated. We are not going to lose anything. We are simply expanding, becoming consciously aware of an even greater depth of ourselves. Moving out of our identification with our identity, our ego, our bodies, we are opening our hearts and minds to the awareness of our true nature.

The experience of our true nature is available to us at any time, as it is always our true nature. It cannot change. We are always a direct expression of one energy, one power, one love; we exist within it and it exists within us. There is no way to change that. There is no way to be outside of God. There is no way to be anything other than God. We muddle our experience with our thoughts and beliefs, but that changes nothing about our true nature. We become so identified with our stories that we believe we have pain, we believe we have lack, we believe we have sickness. None of that impacts the richness, abundance or wholeness of our true nature. It is alive and whole - a God-like being - no matter what we think.

We may think of ourselves as spiritual beings trapped inside a body, doomed to feel pain and frustration. Nothing could be further from the truth. Our incarnation is a blessing, a rare opportunity, a unique experience. We have the potential to experience and know all the attributes of God.

Imagine pure bliss, pure joy, pure love, pure creativity. They are your birthright. They are not lost. They are not hidden. They are alive right at this moment.

You can choose to let go and let the power of those God

attributes rise up within you to cleanse and refresh you. The path is open before you now. Say *yes*. Surrender. Let go. Let the power within you grow. Surrender to it.

18. CHRONIC TENSION

When we have chronic tension - resistance in a part of our body that we don't seem to be able to let go of - it is the expression of the conflict between our desire for freedom and our need to be safe. The desire for freedom is in the here and now, whereas the desire to be safe is an old habit - an old survival mechanism directly linked to the past. The desire to be safe is under the control of the ego and the subconscious mind and so it seems we have no power to release it and let it go. It means that there is a feeling, a state of being, which our body is uncomfortable with, that our ego says is *not good* one way or another, whether it is dangerous or embarrassing, or looks bad, or somehow doesn't match how and who we think we should be. We are maintaining control of our natural energy flows, our natural expression. We are commanding ourselves to fit in, look good, and be safe. The degree to which we will put up this resistance depends on the severity of the response anticipated for letting ourselves express freely.

We must come to understand that what initially caused us to shut down our natural expression was traumatic - in some cases to the degree that it could have been life-threatening. We would not inflict this pain on ourselves without a good reason. We must acknowledge that our response reflects real suffering and deep pain. We acknowledge this not to blame others but so we can be compassionate with ourselves. We must acknowledge this to understand how deeply scared, how terrorized we were, how frightened and alone we were. There is no other reason for us to control ourselves so severely.

We must bring compassion to all of our ideas and thoughts about ourselves; we must forgive ourselves and we must forgive those who inflicted this pain upon us. We must accept what is happening in this moment, not fight or judge it, but see it for what it is – what it really is, not the story about it. In some way, it is beyond our ability to understand. We chose the path to test our ability to remain true to ourselves - to come into our full expression with a depth and breath of understanding and compassion for the existence of pain and suffering. And now our challenge is to become the parents we never had, to become the unconditionally loving and accepting caregivers to ourselves, to give up the judgments and fears, to see the truth of our pain and to acknowledge that it is real. The loss, grief, terror and abandonment are all real in their own way; we cannot pretend that they are not there. Our job is to continue to bring the light of God, the love of God, the unconditional love back into this picture. Our job is to heal and become whole again.

To grieve is to become whole, to restore health, to open up the closed places, to restore the flow of energy. We must soften, have courage and see our fear for what it is - obsolete. We are in no danger. We believe that our grief is a threat and so treat it just as our parents did. We judge it. We are afraid to let go, afraid we will become nothing, afraid we will truly be all alone, afraid there will be no one there for us - and that is indeed how it was. We cannot diminish the truth of our aloneness in that moment.

We know now that there is a bigger truth. There is a God. We know now we are not alone. Somehow we were alone and found ourselves with no one to help. The pain is real. The terror is real. What allowed us to survive was to never feel that again. The cost to our freedom was not considered; our natural instinct was to survive. We couldn't stop ourselves. We would chop off a limb rather than die. The tension or pain we feel is the desperate struggle of that child to continue with their life - to somehow find a way to live in that environment. Be compassionate. See the struggle; see the intensity. Understand. You have all the power of God, all the divine loving nature alive within you; you are the one who can restore the faith and light to this wounded child. You are the one who can remember the truth, who can make the decision to surrender. You know there is either a God or there isn't. You are either perfect or you are not. You choose. Choose to surrender to your perfect, divine self.

19. CHOOSE

When we are not surrendered we are paying attention to our minds. Our ego and our identity are running a constant line of chatter. All the ingrained beliefs, habits, and rules repeat themselves endlessly - stories about ourselves run over and over again. This is what they have been programmed to do throughout our lifetime, and our brain is efficient and does what it is told.

Until we step in and consciously place our awareness on the truth and in the truth, our minds are filled with ceaseless, life-destroying chatter. We become identified with the chatter, we listen to it, we argue with it, we believe it, and yet at the same time the truth is always available to us - a different kind of experience is within us. Our awareness, our consciousness, can be filled with something completely different. It is not just a matter of thinking the right thoughts, although that is helpful. Contemplating the truth, reminding ourselves, is often the first step to opening our mind and focusing our awareness.

When we first affirm and acknowledge who we really are, who

God is, and express gratitude for what we have, both in terms of the material world and in terms of life, then we can begin to remember that there is something bigger inside us. We begin to expand our awareness, to feel and sense our inner experience, to become highly present to what is in us. We become in charge of our mind; we choose what to pay attention to. We choose our thoughts and most importantly, we choose to surrender. We choose in every moment. With our awareness we know there is a presence within us and know we can surrender to that presence. We can relax into the moment and let go of distractions. As we continue to surrender, we let go of any expectations, any ideas, any agenda.

We are merely letting go. That is all we are doing. The truth of our being is always alive within us. The presence of God is always within us. Our true nature is not changed. We are merely removing our obstacles to experiencing it. We are merely letting go of the holding and the resistance. Our only active participation is the decision to let go and keep our mind present and focused: to begin to enter the sacred and holy space, to become present to the light within us. It is alive. We are alive. We continue to let go, to simplify ourselves, to become humble, to become totally present. We agree to surrender, to make room for God.

More often than not, letting go triggers a fear response. We see and acknowledge that fear. We know it for what it is: an old habit of the body. There is nothing to fear. The fear can dissolve; it dissolves in the light as we continue to let go. God is calling us to a deeper experience and our soul longs for this experience – the experience of surrender, freedom, opening, love. It's all here right now. We only need to trust and allow. Let go of holding on. The river is tugging at us, asking us to let go. Do it. Let go.

20. SAY YES

Within you right now is the presence and the voice of God - always available, always there, always vital. What is difficult is to turn the full focus of our attention and awareness inward to what seems like nothing. Our minds are like having a television on in the room. Our attention is constantly drawn to the colors, pictures and sounds. Even though we know we will get no real lasting enjoyment from the television, our attention keeps being called back to it. And though we long for the beautiful peace, bliss, and surrender of remembering who we are, the ego has its own agenda and chatters at us by bringing problems to solve, planning to do, and memories.

We can step back from the ego. When we observe it, we have taken a step away from the hold on our awareness. Now we can become more present. We are in a position to remind ourselves who we truly are. We are not the ego. We are not those thoughts. We are not that personality. We remember that within us and around us is only God, only love, only peace, only stillness. We recognize how we have been holding on, clinging to tiny ideas of ourselves, clinging to our story.

Right now in this moment we are ready to choose to let go, to say *yes* to love, to say *yes* to the power within us, the one power, the only power, the power of creativity and love, of infinite possibilities and potential, of miracles and magic.

This power is alive within you now – right now. Simply turn your attention away from the distractions and there it is: the presence within you - the divine and sacred - the eternal and infinite, unconditionally loving source. It's always here, never judging, never criticizing, ready to support you with all the power in the universe if you will only say *yes*.

But saying *yes* is not simply words. It's an action, a letting go, a surrendering, a melting into God, releasing your grip, opening every channel in your body, unblocking every block. It is only fear that holds you in its grip, but whether you know it or not, what you fear is not what awaits you. Continually say *yes* while acknowledging your mistrust, your doubt and your fear.

Let go of your agenda. Let go of the illusion that you alone are the best chooser of your destiny. Without having complete trust and surrender to God, you cannot possibly choose anything but safety. And when you surrender and let go in this moment you don't have to choose. It's all given to you perfectly, in perfect order and there is no good or bad, right or wrong. There is only the miracle of life, the physical expression of an invisible force called love – the most powerful force in the world – a force that is never overcome by anything. It's all in you right now.

21. THE GAME IS OVER

Consider what lies behind the thoughts you are thinking and the feelings you have in your body. Are the thoughts the source of the feelings or are the feelings the source of the thoughts? Imagine that a dialogue is going on between your mind and your body and you are observing it. You are not the thoughts and you are not the feelings. Who is having those thoughts and feelings? The source of this cycle is apparently an event that took place. But was it really the event? Did the event cause the thoughts and feelings? Did something else cause the thoughts and feelings - a perception, a story, a pattern of thinking, an ingrained belief system activated by a perception?

Although it is often hard to know or see, nothing takes place by accident or coincidence. Everything takes place with further growth and expansion of the human potential. Perhaps we bring perceptions to consciousness to become aware of them so we can use them to heal the wounds, to heal the ways by which we continue to hold limiting and judgmental beliefs about ourselves, and to let them go.

Part of you is hurting and has hurt – felt rejected, abandoned and unworthy - for a long time. It has felt that if the truth about you gets revealed, you will not be wanted. The hurt is there. It is real. But the story around it is not real. A part of you is now ready and stronger than it was in the past. The thoughts you have and your reluctance and inability to let go of them is how you keep hurt at bay. The badness that you feel is the pain of resistance: suppression of yourself, holding yourself down, making yourself small, trying to be invisible. It takes an amazing amount of energy to do that. It tires you out.

You don't have to do that anymore. You can let go of it. What lies within you cannot hurt you or harm you, but resisting can. Allow your heart to open. Allow your compassion to surface. Allow yourself to be an unconditionally loving parent that lives within you. For although it may not fit your story, the purpose of all of your resistance is to try to make yourself lovable. It is to ensure that you do the right thing so you won't be rejected. But the only one that is rejecting you is yourself.

In this moment God is here – holding you with all the love you can imagine. Nothing wrong or bad has happened in the eyes of God. You are not somehow unworthy. There is nothing missing from you. All it takes is for you to acknowledge that part of you that can step out of the story and observe it for what it is. That part of you which knows the truth is willing to accept it as true, despite your conviction that something terrible has happened. You have been hurt; you have been rejected, criticized and abandoned. But that was your human self. It was not your soul, not the spirit within you, not the essence of your being. It was only in time and space - only a test of strengthening.

The game is over. You can remember who you are now. You

have seen through the illusion that you are separate, that you have to do everything yourself, and that you are all alone. Your own divine nature has been revealed to you. You have experienced it and know it is true. It is up to you now to surrender the illusion even more - to bring the light within you into the world. You have the understanding and the compassion of the survivor. Let go now. Let yourself bathe in the light and love that is all around you and within you. Do not punish yourself any longer. Do not hold yourself away from love. Allow yourself to say *yes.* It is there – the light is there. The love is there right now, alive, real, vital.

22. DISTRACTIONS

It is difficult to understand how your ego can do nothing to help you surrender. There is nothing you can do when you are identified with the ego and you believe in the power of your separation, when you believe there is something to improve or to fix or something you can change. This is particularly true when you believe that somehow you are limited or you are not doing enough, not being good enough, not trying hard enough or not doing the right thing. All of this is merely the ego holding on to control.

Every distraction from surrendering is your ego at work, whether it's discomfort in your body, or thoughts in your mind, or feelings. It's all your ego at work, distracting you, holding your attention, keeping you believing in the problems. You believe there is something you have to do before you can surrender, one more thing you have to do. To some degree that is true, but the truth is that you simply have to agree to surrender. You have to agree to give up everything, to let go of everything, to stop trying to change things, to stop trying to improve things.

Your ego is very clever; it's always learning new things. It will not give up of its own accord. As long as you believe there are things to fear, your ego will have power. As long as you accept the idea that you have limits or imperfections, your ego will have power. That is the language of the ego; it's not the language of truth.

What we know is that the truth is alive within you right now and in every moment. The truth is unchanging. Drama - the ego - captivates your attention, distracts you from the truth, but does not change the truth. The truth is still there, still present within you. You distract yourself with issues, worries, problems, limitations and shortcomings. Meanwhile the truth is present within you - unchanging, infinite and eternal. You experience emotional upheavals, tell yourself all kinds of stories, isolate yourself; meanwhile the truth is alive within you.

You think the dramas your mind creates are you, are real, have power, but they are nothing. They don't even exist. They are puffs of smoke that have a few seconds before they dissolve into nothingness. And all the while the truth is present within you, the love is present, the infinite and eternal presence is alive within you and is the source of your being.

You can choose to let go now. You can choose to ignore the fear, the voices in your head, the resistance.

23. THE LIFE FORCE

Although the ego can generate great fear in you, it is not a powerful, dynamic force. In actuality, the powerful, dynamic force is your life, the life force within you. The ego seeks to control and repress this life within you by filling you with fear of rejection and abandonment. The ego is always on guard keeping watch to push down the expression of this life. As powerful as it may seem, it is important to remember that the ego is simply the response of a frightened and overwhelmed child.

The life force, however, can never be completely repressed or suppressed. It is always expressing, always emerging, always flowing. The ego resides in an imaginary world, the world of the physical realm. To the ego, that realm is the only world. The ego's belief that it has power or control over the physical realm is completely false.

The truth is that the life force is expressing in every moment. This universal mind and intelligence is always active and present. It is the only power there is. It's the only truth. It's the only source of movement and flow. It's the only real identity. The ego, by contrast, is not a real identity; it is just a set of conditioned responses. It is a computer program learned by the mind. It has no life of it's own. It is given life by life itself. When that life is withdrawn, it will be gone. But life will go on and that life is alive within you right now and you are alive within it. It has nothing to do with time and space. The ego causes you to feel fear and rage, but the life within you knows peace and love. The ego makes you feel shame and unworthiness, but the life within you knows joy, bliss, and creativity.

Turn your awareness away from your ego - from your thoughts. Feel the presence within you. Surrender and let go. Give up control. Give up holding. Give up the idea that you are responsible for anyone or anyone is responsible for you. Give up the idea that there is something you need to do and that you will do it wrong. Give up the idea that you know what anyone else needs to do.

Within you now is the deep knowing and experience of a perfectly unfolding life, of an infinite, eternal intelligence guiding the unfolding of the universe. There is knowledge of oneness, of the perfection of this moment and every moment. And if you surrender your fear, your resistance, you will be filled with the light. If you give up your need to control, you will remember who you really are. If you allow yourself to fall into openness, to surrender, to sink into the pool, you will dissolve into the oneness that you already are.

There is nothing you need to hold onto, nothing that you need to control. You can open yourself now.

24. MOVE YOUR AWARENESS

Focus, determination, and practice are required to move your awareness away from thoughts of right and wrong and past or future to the present. It also takes understanding of what it means to do nothing, to let go, to surrender. Although focus and determination are required, these qualities are not for *doing* something but instead for remembering not to do - to remember to stop doing. This is more than an activity of the mind; it is a physical letting go, relaxing, becoming still, becoming aware of sensations in your body, becoming aware of the present moment and of what is happening right now. This is the difference between allowing and doing; when you allow something you are actually letting go of stopping it. When you allow yourself to become present, you are simply stopping giving attention to the distractions of your mind and returning your awareness to the present moment.

Make up your mind in this moment to allow whatever is going to happen, to happen. Don't seek to control it in any way. Don't anticipate any kind of experience. Don't measure, analyze, compare; just become present. Letting go is harder than anything else. It's easy to do work, easy to work on ourselves, easy to find problems and analyze them, easy to find solutions. Just sit here right now and let go of control, to allow uncomfortable, painful feelings to come into your consciousness. Overcoming the terror of not being in control is harder than anything you will ever do.

But we *do* do it, we can do it, and we will. When we see the fear and the uncomfortable feelings, we recognize them for what they are. They are the activity of the mind, part of the story. We do not suppress them or deny them. We just let them be. They have no power over us. The feelings are signs of life. They are not indicators that there is something wrong with us, rather they are the movement of energy, of healing, of opening, of surrendering. And so we welcome them.

The driving force of any feeling is love. As long as we deny the feeling we deny the love. Stop holding on. Stop resisting. Allow yourself to soften, to become light, to open your energy system, to open the gates and allow the flow. Give in now to the current. Allow yourself to be carried away and be part of a bigger current. Allow yourself to be held in the field of spirit, the all-encompassing, all-loving, universal source that is the creator of your being in this moment. It surrounds you and fills you. Let go now.

25. GIVE UP TRYING

When we surrender, we are choosing to move the focus of our awareness from our thoughts - our identification with our ego - back to the present, the here and now. When our awareness is occupied with thoughts of the future or the past or with analyzing the present, we are not truly present. The process of moving our awareness back to this moment is threatening to the ego. It is a challenge, and the ego, in any way it can, will continue to distract us from becoming present in the moment.

When we say *I choose to surrender,* asking who is the *I* that is choosing to surrender is a good question. If it is the ego, then our journey is much easier and smoother. We consciously acknowledge our identification with the ego and its desire to protect us with its belief in the need for control. We can acknowledge all that and then acknowledge knowing that there is more to us - there is a greater power within us. We see God as alive within us, a presence in us that is greater than anything else.

We can do this without denying the ego. We can see how we

can agree to what seems like dying to be born again. We can let the ego dissolve. We can agree to be transformed by agreeing to give up any idea about what is best for us, what is coming, who or what we should be.

We can willingly let all this go and accept and trust in the power within us to supply everything we need, to supply all the guidance we need, all our sustenance, all support. We can truly hand over the reins of our lives. There is no longer any need to compare ourselves with others or with what we thought we should be or could be. There is no need to judge and no need to fear.

Once we turn to the presence of God within us and allow that presence to move through us and become our guide, we are truly free. There are no limits to our possibilities. The idea of not being in control is so foreign that it is almost intolerable to the ego. And yet on some deeper level we know that it is the only way. We know that we must trust. We must allow. We must open. We must allow the presence of God within us to be the very fundamental state of being, the basis of our lives, the ground on which we move.

Let go of it all. Let go of everything. There is nothing that you need to hold onto – absolutely nothing. It is time to truly trust, to truly put yourself in the hands of God. It is time to give up trying.

26. IDENTIFICATION WITH EGO

When we are identified with our ego, it feels like our survival is always at risk. It feels like we have problems to solve. It feels like we have shortcomings. But it also feels like we are special, we are better than others. We judge and compare, try to control the future, try to make those around us fit our idea of what they should be. Using a system of conscious and unconscious control of muscular contraction, our energetic system takes on particular configurations based on who we think we are in any given moment. We experience ourselves differently depending on the state of our ego. This is a highly volatile state in which we are sensitive and easily injured. We also seek and welcome praise and reassurance although, superficially, we may reject it.

It is hard to recognize that we are so identified with the ego until we take a step back and make a conscious effort to remember who we are and we observe who we are being in the moment. One thing is certain: when we are identified with the ego we are not present. In fact, we will be resisting anything that suggests we should be present. We will be distracting ourselves in some way, believing the stories of the ego that tell us we have things to do and work to do; we just can't stop to be present. When we give the external world this much power we become victims. We are like leaves getting blown in the wind, swirling around as if we have no power in our own lives.

The illusion of the ego is so complete that we truly believe ourselves to be powerless and, indeed, when we are identified with our ego we *are* powerless because we are always trying to change what is already happening. We are continually trying to rewrite history. We have completely forgotten that we are the source of all that happens. Our observation of what has happened in the outside world is only looking at what happened before instead of what is happening now, observing the past, tinkering with something which has no relevance.

But right now, in this moment, the world is created brand new. There is infinite potential and possibility in every moment – right now, right here – if we will just remember that there is nothing about us that needs to be fixed. We do not need to believe the stories of the ego. We actually need to have an energetic shift so we can become aware of this moment, start to let go of the constant noise and chatter of our mind, start to turn within, and start to remember the truth about ourselves. We allow ourselves to relax, to let go of the tension, to let go of holding the contractions and blocked energy in our body. It becomes so comfortable when we are not identified with the ego.

27. CONTROL

It's not difficult to understand why it's hard for us to let go, to surrender, to trust in God. When we were dependent on those around us to protect us, to make us safe and to look after us, our trust was deeply betrayed. As time passed we developed strategies to look after ourselves and keep ourselves safe. However, to do this meant we had to give up a large part of our self-expression.

We believed that the only way we could keep ourselves safe was to begin to exert control over ourselves and our environment. We tightened so determinedly that we lost consciousness of the extent of our control. Eventually it became a habit to the point where, even if we could become conscious of it, the idea of letting go was frightening. The results of losing control felt like death. We made up our mind to not feel fear anymore, to not need anyone, to never count on anybody. We decided that we didn't need anybody because we could do it all on our own. The terrible dilemma of this is that we can never be free to experience the full expression of our being while we maintain that tight control, that habitual structure.

To free ourselves we need to face the pain and fear once again - which is almost unthinkable. There is a difference now. We are not the dependent, vulnerable child, and on some level we now know that we are not alone.

Our ego asserts itself strongly against any form of surrender or loss of control. Its job has been to keep us functioning in a way that is safe from the overwhelming feelings of fear and abandonment. Now the path to freedom, to joy and to liberation lies through the release of all that holding and coming face to face with the pain and fear, to finally let it go.

We will not be overcome. We will not be destroyed. We will not die. We have all we need to make the journey back to the full expression of our being. We are not alone. We are safe. We are not powerless. We are not victims. We are not what our ego tells us we are: we are not weak, stupid, slow, inadequate, or undeserving. We are children of God.

We are endowed with the ability to create miracles. We are indeed miracles ourselves in every moment. Our life, this life, this experience is a miracle. Our very existence is a miracle. If you begin to list all the processes that are happening in your body right this minute - the trillions of cells that are working intelligently, the incredible complexity of your nervous system, the inner dependency on your environment, all the ways you have of receiving information, all the things that you don't even know you know, all the intelligence that it takes to make this body work - you can see how truly miraculous our existence is.

Yes, the pain is intense and the fear is overwhelming. But there is nothing bigger than the power of God. There is nothing that can destroy it or even hurt it. That power is alive within you right in this moment. That love flows through you right now and in every moment. There is nothing you can't do or be. Allow yourself to rest. Give up being on the alert. Give up the watchfulness, the tension. Allow yourself to take a break from trying to do or be anything. Give up using your will. Surrender your control.

Just let go. Surrender into the embrace of the universal, divine and loving spirit within you. It surrounds you and fills you. It will support you in every moment. Let go. Let go now. God is already taking care of your life. Everything is already unfolding without your control.

28. ABUNDANCE

I know that the first step in opening myself to the true abundance of the universe is forgiving myself for having believed in lack, for having believed all the stories that became part of my story as I grew up – stories involving stress, tension, despair, hopelessness, and all the negative emotions around money. I took them on. I couldn't help it. They were in the air, as part of the environment in which I grew up. It became part of my story. And now I acknowledge the degree to which I took that story on and made it my own. I believed in lack, I believed in unworthiness, I believed there was a link between how hard I worked and how much I had. I believed it was all up to me. I believed so many things I now know weren't true.

And I now forgive myself. I accept myself and I release all these old beliefs and stories. I release the fear, anxiety and all the negative beliefs about money. I'm letting them go now. Now I know money is not bad. It is not evil. It's not a source of stress or a source of negative feelings, and it's not the cause of anger, depression or fear. That is not what money does. That is what stories do. I'm releasing those stories now. I don't need them anymore. They are not part of my new way of being with money.

My new way of being with money is recognizing that money is a positive force. It is an energy. It carries with it power and that power can create, support and manifest all kinds of good things. That power is part of the energetic flow of abundance that is unlimited, which has never been limited, which has always been infinite and eternal. Only I, through my insistence on it being limited - on it being stressful - have caused any lack of abundance in my life. And now I let go. I forgive myself completely for that. I accept myself. I understand and acknowledge that now I can change. I can be different with money now.

I love the power, the freedom, the fun, the enjoyment that money brings into my life. I love the good, the beauty, the opportunities to share, support, help, and grow. So much more opens up to me because I value the good that money brings. I allow that abundance to flow into my life now. I am no longer insisting that I have to know where it comes from. It can come from anywhere. I don't have to know how to make it appear. God can take care of all that.

Miracles and magic are real. They are true. They happen all the time. I am going to allow them to happen to me. I am going to allow miracles and magic into my life. I now allow myself to embrace the magic of options, opportunities, and choice. I now know that I have the ability to do what I want to do - what I need to do, what I choose to do, what I see to do.

I am never, ever going to allow myself to be limited because I don't believe in abundance or miracles. I am now opening to all of the beauty and love, inspiration and abundance that God intended for me in the beginning, the life that has been available to me right from the beginning. Now I'm opening to it. I am not going to block it anymore.

I am going to be free wherever I am, whether I'm shopping, working, supporting, helping or sharing. Whatever I'm doing I will be free. I will. I see the good. I feel the joy and the freedom, the opportunities to buy what I want. I don't have to hold back. I don't have to look at the price tag. I shop for what is beautiful, what is appropriate, what is perfect - for what I want. I can afford whatever I want. I shop because I love it. Everything in my life that involves money is done because it is perfect. I support people because it is perfect to support them. I share because it is perfect to share. I bring beauty. I support beauty. I do all of that now because I am free from all my limiting beliefs about money. I am letting them go. I forgive myself. Money is now my friend. It is everybody else's friend too.

29. FEAR OF DEATH

To make the transition from identification with the ego, to identification with our true self requires letting go of any idea that there is an action to take, that there are problems to solve, that there is anything wrong. The body must move from the survival mode into creative mode utilizing two completely different nervous systems.

When we still believe in the fears, the injuries, the wounds, and the stories of the past, our ego – supervisor of our survival mode - is ready to fight or ready to flee. It is prepared for disaster. At these times we are in the grip of survival mode, with no interest in the quality of life - no interest in whether we are happy or miserable. The ego's only goal is to keep us alive at any cost. It is hardwired. People are known to sever limbs or take other extreme measures to stay alive. Living from survival gives no guarantees about the quality of life.

When we let go of our view of the world as a dangerous or difficult place, when we understand truly and deeply that our survival is not at stake - that there is no death and that the quality of our life is more important than mere survival - we can move out of the survival mode into acceptance, understanding, and then into creativity, and a deep experience of our true selves.

Our greatest fear in survival mode is death. And so we must accept the possibility of our own death as a consequence of letting go of the survival mode. We must look at that fear squarely and say, *I am prepared to accept that consequence.* Each time we meditate we face dying, and we do die in one way: we give up the fight, the battle for survival and let go of the need to survive at any cost. What may not be so clear to us is that our desire to look good, to fit in, to avoid humiliation, springs from the fear of death - the fear of abandonment. It all comes down to that.

Once you have experienced your infinite self, some part of you will never forget it. Some part of you is there to remind you, *yes, indeed, you will never die.* Just the very fact of acknowledging that gives you more power than you ever had in survival mode.

And so we acknowledge the fear that keeps us struggling - the fear of death, which ironically brings us closer to death than we need be. We understand that we can survive in this world without fear, that we have infinite possibility at our disposal if we will simply allow and trust. We have seen plenty of evidence of it. How could we not acknowledge the miracles and synchronicities that happen constantly?

What is the worst thing that could happen if you let go right now - if you totally surrendered to the peace and love within you? The ego has a very disturbing idea of what would happen but you know that's not true. You know that what would happen is that you would be filled with love and light, that you would experience the joy and peace of your oneness with God. Do you prefer holding on, to prevent the disaster the ego presents?

All your life you have feared losing control and now it is what you most long to do – to be free, to be in love, to have power, to create, to heal, to experience true joy and peace, to truly experience the nature of your oneness with God. Let go now. Let go of the need to survive and welcome the joy of life.

30. IMAGINATION

As you relax and let go of all the activities of your mind, as you focus on the present and what's real in this moment, you fall deeply within yourself and you begin to remember that within you is a place of deep peace and contentment, an environment of knowing that everything is perfect, that everything is fine. Can you allow that knowing, that peace, to arise within you, into your awareness, into your experience? Just allow yourself to experience peace. Allow yourself to feel that everything is perfect. You don't need to engage your mind; this happens on a feeling level and has nothing to do with your thoughts. Peace comes when we experience ourselves in this moment - right now. Peace comes when we let go and allow it.

All that we experience as non-peace is the activity of our mind. It's our activity in time and space. It's measuring our lives by actions in time. Yet, even while we are engaged in doing that, even while we are distracted, peace is still real, still present, still true and still perfect.

If you knew the countless billions of processes that happen every day to support your life, if you really grasped the amazing miracle that your life is, the enormity of evolution, the complexity, of cooperation between systems, if you really grasped that, grasped the miracle that you are, your anxieties and worries would seem trivial. They indeed are trivial. The power of the intelligence that is at work to keep you alive in this moment is so unimaginably vast, so complex, so intelligent - and this power at work within you wants you to live.

You are not some accident of nature; you are not some random chance event. You have not been put here to be tested, to see if you measure up, to be tortured or to be made to suffer. You are a unique aspect of a divine and infinite intelligence coming to know itself by way of you. This divine intelligence, this infinite power has placed all of its power in you by its very infinite nature. It can withhold nothing from you; it can only give.

Now, by surrendering, letting go of being in charge, of being in control, letting go of everything that is not God, you bring that power to bear in your life - you bring miracles, synchronicities, potential and possibilities that are truly magic beyond your imagining. It's all within you right now. You can allow it. You can dream it into being. You can imagine it into being and believe it into being. Nothing will ever be created in your life that you are not in agreement with. Your life is effect. It is not cause.

It is easy for the ego to discount the possibilities of change, to ridicule ideas, to resist magic, to remind you over and over again of how many times you have failed. You can count on your ego to do that. But why would you listen to it when you know that there is a law at work that is impossible to contradict? Why do you want to live as if you are somehow exempt from the workings of that law?

If your ego were another person in your life, you would not want to be around them. Not that they would be bad or evil, but they would be too focused on lack, failure, and limitation. The ego has no imagination, creativity, or love. And yet we rely on our ego for guidance most of the time. We listen to it, we believe it, we act on its guidance even though we have available to us all the intelligence and wisdom, all the love and knowledge, all the creativity and imagination that ever existed, within us right now. But we must choose. We are not victims in any moment; we always have the power of choice. In any moment we can remind ourselves: *I know that I am a unique and beautiful aspect of God. I know that within me in this moment is all the power, creativity, beauty, intelligence and wisdom of God. I know I can trust this power within me; I can trust this loving source within me. I know that miracles and magic are possible in any moment. I know that every limitation I feel is merely a function of ego and has nothing to do with reality. I know that every resistance I feel, every fear I feel is trivial compared to the power of God within me.*

Let God do the work for you. Let God guide the way. There is so much power at your disposal. God has no interest in hard work, suffering, misery. With no effort whatsoever, but only divine intention, God creates this universe right now, right here. With no effort, that divine intention is expressed through you right now. All that creative power is expressed through you right this moment. There is no requirement for difficulty. It's only your mind that imagines limits. God does not imagine limits.

Commit yourself to allowing miracles, to surrendering your limitations to infinite, creative power, to using your imagination to create peace instead of misery. Your imagination is your greatest gift. Use it. Your imagination is your doorway to miracles. Set it free. Set yourself free.

31. SURVIVAL

When we were very young children we had a great need to
know that we were loved. It is built into our genetic code that
if we are not loved we are at risk. But how did we know if we
were loved? How does a child know if they are loved? A child
knows because love is an energy they can feel. Love is a
fundamental aspect of our being; it is the life-giving force.

When we are open and surrendered, we feel love. We feel love
for and from others. This is a basic survival mechanism that is
built into us. But we have other survival mechanisms. When
we begin to realize that our parents aren't openly giving love,
these other mechanisms kick into place, forcing us to use our
minds and brains in ways that were designed for emergency
use only. And so we live our lives from childhood on as if we
are constantly responding to emergencies. This wears us out.
It brings no satisfaction and becomes a very highly rule-bound
and structured way of living. We become convinced that we
are alone, that we have to manage everything by ourselves and
that there is no place for us. We don't open our hearts
anymore because we are terrified that nothing will be there.

We have spent a considerable amount of time trying to understand how we came to be the way we are. We have had many experiences. We understand that it is time for us to open our hearts; it's time for us to trust. It's time for us to move out of emergency survival and into enjoyment and fulfillment and the creative use of an incredible faculty - consciousness. But the fear is structured in us; it's habitual. We long to surrender, we yearn for freedom and peace, yet letting go of fear seems so difficult.

We forget how far we have come because our desire for freedom is so great. Every moment of not having it seems like an eternity. We forget that we do have moments when we experience the complete unconditional love that is alive within us. We do have moments where we experience the complete peace of knowing who we are. We do have moments of being truly in the flow of divine creativity. So we know for a fact what we long for is possible.

But our old habits die hard. It only takes a moment to slip back into emergency mode where when we perceive a threat to our identity. One trigger and the old habit kicks back in. When this happens we must begin the process of surrendering and letting go once again. It may sound tiresome and difficult and sometimes it seems too hard. It is in these times that the ego feels most threatened. The ego still has us convinced that it is hard work to surrender, that we won't achieve it, that it's a waste of time. But it is not. It's not hard work. There is nothing hard about surrendering except facing the fear - except trusting in the face of fear.

All the difficulty takes place in the realm of thought. This is why we divert our attention away from the realm of thought and become diligent in our intention and commitment to remembering who we are. From this place we can surrender to awareness, to the observer, to the sensor, to the one who experiences the sensations of being alive. Not the one who analyzes and gives meaning to them, but the one who experiences them, and is aware in this moment of every sensation - the one who does nothing but be aware.

It is from this state of awareness - simple beingness - that we open to the presence of God within us. In this state our hearts can open to the presence of love within us and our minds can open to infinite intelligence. We slip out of the realm of time and space into the eternal now and can realize our own true nature, our oneness, our infinite and eternal oneness.

32. FEAR

There is a tendency to believe that when we feel fear it means we shouldn't go ahead with whatever we are doing. Fear is given some kind of credibility as a determinant for following a course of action. We have come to believe in fear, to have faith in fear, as if it somehow knows what we should or shouldn't do. We think our choices should be guided by fear - that we should allow fear to determine what we do and don't do. We feel that a determination based on fear is a good enough reason to make the choices that we make.

It is important for us to realize that fear arises in the world of effects and not in the world of cause. Although it has a very real role in survival, our survival is rarely at stake; when we hand our lives over to the world of first cause we very rarely encounter circumstances that threaten our survival. But our ego remembers all too well on a body level, what is threatening. And what we are most afraid of is our own life force. There are certain ways that we are frightened to death of having our life force expressed - the ways that led us to be faced with the prospect of abandonment, humiliation, punishment, or pain.

So our mode of survival is to turn against the Life Force in our body, to suppress it, control it, deny it and to feel fear when it threatens to break through. Now we can understand the greatest fear of all is losing control. To avoid this loss of control, the ego is dire in its warnings about the idea of letting go. It is skilled and adept at making us fear the loss of control more than anything. So we know that when we feel fear, our survival is not at stake, rather our ego is hard at work convincing us that being free is not a good thing. We believe that free expression in our lives can only lead to disaster and feeling awful or terrible consequences. It is paralyzing to know on another level that we want so badly to be free, while being convinced that there is some awful consequence to our freedom.

When we are immobilized by fear and cannot seem to take the next step, we can summon a deeper understanding - a higher perspective of who we are and why the fear is coming. We can disengage from the ego and turn to our higher power. We can become the functioning adult in the face of the primal terror of the ego. We do not want to deny or suppress the fear; we want to acknowledge and accept it, understand it, and be compassionate toward it. The terrified child inside us needs comforting, not punishment or judgment. Once we find compassion and understanding, our heart can open and the fear is dissolved.

The fear is merely the absence of love, faith and trust. Fear is not a power of its own. It is not a force. It is the absence of a force for good. A person feels fear when they have no one to turn to when they have been abandoned and they have closed the pathways to their own inner wisdom, their own life force, and are left totally on their own. But we know that we are not alone and are not separate. There is no separation. We must affirm the truth in our minds, the truth that is stronger than any fear, the truth that opens our mind to a new awareness. So call it what you will - affirming the truth, praying, denial, or treatment. Start remembering who you are even if it means reading or repeating line after line of a prayer. Do not do it to deny, suppress, or ignore how you feel. Do it to bring comfort, truth, nurturing and guidance – to heal, not punish. Become clear about the truth; hold it in your mind.

The ego constantly tells us that the solutions to problems are in the world - that is where we should be looking for answers. To counterbalance that constant message remind yourself of the absolute truth - that there is no separation from God. There is no power in evil. There is nothing wrong. There is no imperfection or defect in you. You are not missing anything. You have access to the same power as anyone else, including God. There are no contradictions to this truth. There are no exceptions. That is why it is law - because it is always true. Anytime we act in a way that denies or contradicts this truth we are acting from the ego and that only strengthens and reproduces the fear, and ensures that it will continue.

You cannot convince God that you are somehow imperfect or less deserving, unworthy or inadequate. There is nothing you can do to become less than perfect. All you can do is act like you are imperfect and experience the consequences of that act. The result will be to reinforce your own belief in your imperfection. You can always prove to yourself that you are imperfect by acting as if you are. That has nothing to do with truth. That is the world of secondary cause. You do not surrender because you are afraid; you do because if you don't surrender your fear becomes more powerful. Ironically, if you

do surrender, fear dissolves. Surrender now. Trust God. Feel
the fear, acknowledge it, reassure it, and surrender. Do it again
and again.

33. LOVING OURSELVES

We often hear how important it is to love ourselves. But in the context of knowing the truth of who we really are - which is unconditional love - how do we love ourselves? What does that mean? Who is doing the loving of whom? It seems apparent that God is not waiting for our love, so loving ourselves must refer to loving the ego or the identity - the way we like to think of ourselves. It is true that the ego is generally not loving in the messages it gives us; its view of who we are seems to hold something very different from loving. One has to question whether the ego is capable of loving at all. We can hold the picture of ourselves as loving or we could hold the picture of loving ourselves, but both are what we like to believe about ourselves: an identity. So how can we truly love ourselves?

When we see someone who has been hurt, whether physically or emotionally, unjustly or through no fault of his or her own, we feel a strong sense of compassion for them. Our heart opens, tears may come to our eyes, or we may feel anger for their unjust treatment. Overall what is triggered is a heart opening, a bonding, a connection, a desire to join with that person to soothe and replenish their self-worth.

And yet when we see this in ourselves, we hold nothing but judgment and contempt. We are the perpetrators of our own injures and wounds. We continue the work that was started early in our childhood. By doing so we continually reinforce the idea that we are inadequate, unworthy or undeserving. Though we are mostly aware of the injury or inadequacy, we are also aware - even if it is unconscious - that we are the one who continues to keep that wound open, continues to keep reinforcing that injury. On some level we are well aware of how badly we treat ourselves. We may not be conscious of it, but deep down we know.

Nevertheless, the concept of loving ourselves generates ideas of forgiveness, compassion, understanding, nurturing, caring, allowing. We are so much more tolerant of those that we care about than we are with ourselves. We find one instance of failure on our part and punish ourselves mercilessly. And yet we tirelessly support our friends and children no matter how much they fail.

So how do we bring compassion to ourselves? It starts with our intention to remember who we are. Even if we do not feel the presence of God within us in any moment, there is a part of us that knows the truth. We are not just ego or pure love; we are conscious beings with a self-awareness. We can be aware of ourselves as God or we can be aware of ourselves as identity, or we can be aware of ourselves as compassionate, loving, expressions of God's divine wisdom and unconditional love, whether we feel connected to it or not. Even if we cannot feel a connection we can still remember that that's who we are. To do this takes intention, vigilance, and commitment.

There is a greater understanding alive within you. You know the truth. The fact that you get separated from it, that you aren't consciously aware of the presence within you, does not diminish the truth. This is the key understanding for you: forgive yourself and let go of your identity along with your ego, and become compassionate, understanding and forgiving. In effect, you are refining your identity and your ego to be in line with the truth. You are correcting them so that they are not working against your knowing who you are.

At the moment it is too easy for you to say, *I have this wound or this injury that has caused me to be disabled in this way or that.* What you are not understanding is that it is you who keeps the wound or injury alive by repeating that statement.

If you were to say, *I am not this injury or this wound; I am perfect unconditional love, an expression of God, and could not possibly be less than perfect,* it would change your mind completely. All this emerges from compassion, understanding and forgiveness, being gentle and kind with yourself. You may notice a sense of repugnance at the concept of being gentle and kind with yourself. Take note of that. It is important. Most of us do not feel that we deserve to be treated with kindness and gentleness. We feel that we need discipline, harsh measures, hard work and pain to get us where we are going.

All the power, all the love, all the beauty of God is in you right now - the power to heal anything, completely, perfectly and forever is available in this moment. This is the truth. This is the absolute truth of who you are. You have the power to create miracles of any proportion. Do not fool yourself any longer, that you are somehow disempowered or disabled. Be kind, be gentle, be compassionate. Train yourself to think kindly about yourself. This is how we move into alignment with the truth.

When you meditate and surrender you remember the truth, but it is not always easy to take that memory into your daily life because your ego and identity are not aligned with the truth. There is a deep wisdom and intelligence within you - an aware, conscious being with choices. Activate that being now. Be in charge of your mind. Correct it's thinking. Do not accept the victimhood and powerlessness of your ego and your identity.

Remember that despite anything you may feel or believe at any given moment, there is much power within you. All of the infinite potential of the universe exists within you; all of the divine wisdom and infinite intelligence and unconditional love is alive in every aspect of your being in this moment. The kingdom of God is alive within you. It is yours now. The gifts of the kingdom are yours. They are with you forever. You can never lose them. You can never use them up. You are blessed with the kingdom of God forever.

34. THE DAM IS BREAKING

Resistance is like a dam. We become aware of resistance
because it is holding back the flow of energy. The purpose of
the dam is to contain certain movements of energy called
emotions, which were perceived to be a threat to survival.
There were some forms of expression that were not welcome
in our family and we quickly learned to block them, usually on
a subconscious level but sometimes consciously. In the end it
all became subconscious because of habit; a structure was built
to keep those dangerous feelings unexpressed. The problem
that we have now is that that dam blocks all feelings. It doesn't
let some emotions through and not others. All energetic
motion is blocked. This is uncomfortable. It consumes energy.
It blocks the life-giving force. It reduces our vitality. And in the
end, it usually causes some kind of dysfunction in the body
because the vital energy is trapped and blocked.

The good news is that the dam is not made of concrete; it is
made of sand. As we tire of our unfulfilled lives and begin to
work with the resistance, we open up cracks in the dam. Like
any dam made of sand, the movement of energy begins to

break down the dam. And every time we release an old trapped emotion, another crack is created in the dam and more energy flows through. At some point the momentum of the flowing energy is greater than the ability of the dam to hold it.

There is a part of us that is working on holding the dam back in place, throwing sand back into the cracks trying to shore it up. And so sometimes the cracks are temporarily repaired. But that part of us is insubstantial compared to the light and the power available to us when we surrender to our true nature and allow God to do the work.

What it means to let God do the work confuses us. We are so used to having to figure out what to do - how to take care of ourselves, the next step. We cannot imagine how to hand that over. We have been responsible for so much for so long that it seems impossible to let go of that responsibility. We may have a great fear that if we hand that work over to God, nothing will happen – that God is not really interested in us and we are irrelevant. This is part of our story.

The truth is that God has never abandoned us. We turned away from God. There is no way for God to abandon us for there is only God. Our human selves, confused and overwhelmed by our childhood situations, were forced to make decisions that would exclude trust in God – not because we had been betrayed by God but because we had been let down by our parents.

Now we come to this point with the idea of handing our healing and our lives over to God. It's such an unlikely prospect. It brings out a strong response from our ego - that part of us that believes our survival depends on staying in control. And so we have a dilemma, a dilemma created by our longing for freedom, peace, health, and prosperity, pitted against our inability to surrender to that which will give us all of that. We have the dilemma of our absolute determination to stay in control versus our innermost longing for connection and love. What we may not know or may have forgotten is that when we stop, surrender, open our minds and hearts, our way is clear. What we need appears before us. What we want is given to us. We are guided by a loving, divine intelligence that cannot make mistakes.

This loving, divine intelligence has been with us since the beginning. It has been guiding us from the beginning. This may seem unlikely, but our evolution into conscious self-awareness of this divine power within us required the journey we made. There was not one part of it that could have been different. There may be a lot of it that we don't understand, but we will. And that is our goal: the conscious awareness, experience, and use of the divine power within us in order to become the creator we are capable of being. We are not wounded animals, healing from victimization. We are powerful, divine beings, being born into our own power.

Through the struggles of our human nature we are freeing our divine nature. We are not proving inadequacy; we are not coping with limitation. We are overcoming challenges and obstacles that are creating powerful beings of creativity, love and light. And that is the purpose for our lives. Our struggle begins when we believe that we are merely human. Our struggle dissolves in the light of our divine nature.

Our challenge becomes identifying with our divine nature, to become the loving presence that gives us life. We must give up our attachment to our human story and our identification with duality, and accept the gifts and treasures that are our divine birthright. We must let go of the judgments of ourselves. We have never failed; we have overcome overwhelming obstacles. We have become more and more conscious. There are substantial cracks in the dam and light is flooding through.

We know that there is one God, one power. We know this in the depths of our being. We know that we are meant for more than what our ego would have us live. We know that. We have always known that. We have always known that we were one with God. It's always been there calling us back, guiding us, steering us, supporting us, providing just what we needed when we needed it. We are divine beings. We are filled with light, love and a creative power beyond all imagining.

Stop and become still. We now know that we can surrender, we will surrender. We are safe. We can trust. We can let go. In this moment there is great love for you. Give in to it. Soften your heart. Give in to the divine power within you. The loving presence of light is alive within you right now. Nothing that happened in your past makes any difference now. The only thing that matters is this moment and whether you choose to surrender. When you choose to surrender, the world of possibility opens before you.

35. EVERYTHING IS OKAY

Most of us are familiar with the feeling of having some important task to do in the future that creates some anxiety or doubt about our ability to complete. We worry that it will have undesirable effects, such as giving people a bad opinion of us, or not being able to actually do what we were supposed to do. On one hand, we dread the negative aspects of the coming task, but, on the other hand, there may be other aspects that excite us about it. And then the time comes and we do the task, we do it well, we receive good feedback, and we return home with a tremendous sense of burden lifted, knowing that we no longer have that weighing on our mind.

This is, in actuality, the same feeling most of us experience at some point in every day of our lives. There is an underlying anxiety, fear or dread about something that is coming or something that has passed. There is some belief in something awful, whether it's lack or humiliation, inadequacy, abandonment or rejection. We spend much of our time in anticipation of something awful. Much of this is habitual and below the level of conscious awareness.

What we should have learned by now is that rarely does something turn out as badly as we expect or imagine it will. When we experience the feeling of having completed a task and having the burden lifted from our shoulders, the relief, the peace, the feeling of an open future without that burden, we are feeling the feeling of surrendering to our true nature. We realize deep within that everything is okay, has always been okay, always will be okay. We recognize that we are okay, and just as good as anyone else.

There is nothing that can actually impair the perfection of the spirit within you. There is nothing that can limit the power available to you except your own belief in limitations. Imagine that feeling when thinking that something terrible has happened and then finding that everything is okay. You realize that you were just imagining it - it wasn't ever real. It was just your thoughts that made it real, and you find out it was never true. Imagine the feeling of relief, lightness, everything being okay.

Any time you think something is wrong you are imagining it. It may not be so obvious that everything is okay but the purpose of your spiritual journey is to make that your reality. We are not trying to become better people. We're not trying to improve ourselves. We're not trying to fix something that is broken. We're simply trying to remember the truth.

Imagine how your body relaxes, your mind surrenders, imagine enjoying the feeling of relief when finding that everything is okay, that there's nothing wrong, there's no danger. Allow yourself to feel that now. Allow yourself to imagine feeling that everything is okay - that there is nothing to worry about. Just imagine it. Don't listen to the ego that will raise all sorts of complaints. There are no complaints.

What the ego says is simply the ego attempting to retain control. It is not truth. Imagine that everything is okay. It is safe to do that. No harm will come to you. You are not being foolish. You are actually aligning yourself with the deepest reality, the only reality. Do that now. Imagine that. Imagine that everything is all right. Imagine that you have an intelligence within you that can never let you down - that knows everything, that is creative and has a solution for every problem. Just imagine that. What does that feel like to know that you will never be stuck for a solution? That the answers will always come? How does that feel? Really feel that you will always have an answer. Imagine that your needs will always be met. Don't listen to your ego. Just imagine that your needs will always be met. What does it feel like to know that you will never have to worry? What does it feel like to know that your abundance is overflowing and can never run out? How does that feel - because it is the truth. How does it feel to know that whatever opportunities you desire, there are endless possibilities in every moment for creating those opportunities? How does it feel to know that you will always have the opportunities you desire?

You may notice resistance to feeling these feelings and imagining these scenarios. This is the ego at work. This is the degree to which you are not experiencing reality. For none of the considerations that have been posed are outside of reality. It is the truth. Everything you hear in your mind that counteracts that truth is illusion, powerless, an habitual and limiting way of thinking.

You can realign with reality by insisting on the truth, by taking the mind away from that resistance and placing it on the truth. As you focus on the truth, allow yourself to feel it. Allow yourself to feel the relief of knowing that everything is unfolding perfectly, that you are safe, and all your needs are met. There is nothing you lack. Feel that. Feel the relief. Surrender to that knowledge. Anything else is a denial of the truth.

All the answers you require are within you now. You can relax. The struggle is over. There is an eternal and infinite truth that is alive within you now. What you have been looking for is found. Allow that idea, that truth, to penetrate your very being. Allow yourself to experience that truth through every cell of your body. Just allow it. Imagine it. You are free. Your life is a perfect expression of the intelligence and love within you. You are not alone. You never were. You never will be. Allow the deep peace and surrender to the truth to fill you. Allow yourself to relax and melt into the knowledge and experience of yourself as being free, powerful and infinite. Just let yourself go.

36. YOUR BODY IS THE MIRROR

Chances are that, in this moment, you are holding on in some way to a block in your energy - some kind of habitual holding pattern that keeps you tied to the survival mode. The holding on is a defensive reaction, a defense against the movement of energy that threatens the ego's control. When we talk about letting go and surrendering, we are talking about an actual physical process as well as an attitude. The action transition from survival to creation is a physical process and an energetic one, which is why there are physical exercises such as yoga to help the *letting go* process.

When our holding is habitual and has been going on for most of our lives, it is very difficult to be aware of it. Until this holding – or resistance - manifests as pain or symptoms, as weaknesses in bones or joints, we don't really notice it. But as we make our journey of letting go and surrendering more deeply to our true nature, we become aware of our resistance manifesting as chronic blocks that seem intractable - though they are not.

Our habit is to believe that there is something wrong with us when we encounter these seemingly intractable blocks, pains and other manifestations of blocked energy. Our first response is to judge them, to feel inadequate, to decide that there is something wrong with us, to feel hopeless or helpless – all kinds of habitual patterns are triggered.

With this first response, we often attempt to resist this resistance, to force against it, to push it, to try to break it - in other words - to engage it, to empower it, to give it more power than it actually has. In fact, resistance doesn't actually have power; we use our own power to strengthen resistance. This is not to say that we don't work with our resistance to gain consciousness and awareness. The important thing to know is that our resistance to the resistance drags the battle on even longer than it needs to be.

When we accept ourselves exactly as we find ourselves in any moment, when we can express compassion for ourselves, when we truly accept *what is* in the moment knowing that all things are possible, our evolution is assured, and our perfection is already established, working *with* our resistance becomes a totally different experience.

The first thing we often forget is that we are divinely guided in every aspect of our lives. Nothing has happened by accident. There is a perfection about our path that our view is too limited to completely understand. We have not been selected to suffer. We are not somehow broken and unable to heal. We are not special in our woundedness. But our ego insists that we are special, that somehow it's harder for us, somehow others are luckier, others are more – or less - advanced than we are. We have all kinds of stories to prove that it is harder for us than most.

In order to maintain this position we must constantly be judging and analyzing. In order to judge, we must judge everything, for judging is a frame of reference. This is a frame of reference that says there is good and bad, right and wrong - duality. It is true that duality seems to exist in the physical world. It is hard to see through it. Nevertheless, we know it is an illusion. We know there is no reality. We know there is only one power. We know this power is infinite. We know it is good and nothing can be outside of it. We know that.

Yet we insist that somehow, we are an exception. Somehow, we are the unique case. Somehow, it is a little bit more difficult for us to surrender, to let go, to be happy, to experience joy, than it is for other people.

We forget that everything that has occurred so far, that has brought us to this point, was absolutely necessary. We forget that this particular experience called being human has been perfectly unfolding in ways which we may not see yet, in ways which we will never understand if we continue to view them through the lens of duality. In truth the *real you* is completely untouched by events in your life.

You spend much time trying to make your human life as comfortable as possible, forgetting that you have all the power of the universe at your disposal, forgetting that there is nothing wrong in any way, forgetting that everything is already perfect and that any discomfort you have is a result of your refusal to accept that. You are not in pain or suffering because there is something wrong with you. It's because you are afraid to trust and let go. If you take pills for your pain you will get more pain. If you battle cancer you will lose.

Your body is merely the mirror of your connection with God.

The extent to which your body is sore or ill is the extent to which you don't trust God. Working on your body will not help you to trust God. Having a perfect body will not make you trust God any more than you already do. The resistance you feel right now anywhere in your body is not telling you to work with it, to engage with it, to empower it. It's telling you to let go of something.

We have a habit of nurturing our weaknesses - of attaching to them. What we want to do is let go of them. With determination and intent we can let go of anything very quickly if we are prepared to face the fear of letting go - of losing control. We must understand that our attachment to our physical symptoms is actually our refusal to face our fear of letting go.

When we were young, experiences in life that were overwhelming and too awful, caused us to contract and hold - to block energy movement. The ego was built on this structure of holding, protecting, and denying. A complicated system of beliefs around our energy was imprinted so that now we are afraid of our own life force. We are afraid to open up and let ourselves be truly alive.

There is no judgment in this. There is no scale of value whatsoever. It simply is what it is. It is a natural process that enabled us to survive - that strengthened us. But now that natural process is the source of our suffering. Our fear of being overwhelmed, our fear of humiliation, of abandonment and rejection is the source of all of our suffering. When we blame our suffering on the body, we betray the truth.

When we are on a spiritual path we take responsibility for our lives. We have committed ourselves to expansion of our awareness and consciousness so that we become free in our expression of who we truly are. And now, on our journey, we must accept ourselves as perfect. We are not to judge, and instead, understand our suffering as temporary and completely unnecessary any longer. We are not victims of our egos. We have been hypnotized but we have experienced and tasted the truth and can no longer deny its validity. We are not asleep; we are awake. We know we have the capacity for joy, peace and freedom. We can surrender and let go. We can trust in our own divine heritage, our birthright. We can surrender now, let go of control, let go of our fascination with our ego, with our suffering, with our problems. We can turn our awareness to our true nature. We can empty our awareness, to be still and let go.

Now is the time to move from serving the ego to surrendering your life to the service of the divine within you. You cannot serve two masters.

37. UNIQUELY YOU

When we are ready to surrender, it's not unusual for us to experience conflict, distraction, or some kind of difficulty. No matter how much we affirm the truth it seems that the opposite of the truth is affirming itself within us. In these cases it is often true that there are strong emotions present that may be more or less unconscious. We may be feeling fear, anger or grief and that fear in our body conflicts with our attempts to believe that everything is okay. We have learned to judge our feelings and use them as warning signals that something is wrong.

There was a time when we thought our feelings were dangerous. This conflicts with experiencing these emotions and with believing that everything is okay. But that is exactly what we must do. We must learn to take away the judgment and to become present and aware of our inner processes. A large part of our difficulty in surrendering is that we are denying or suppressing the feelings we have. Denying or suppressing emotions is an act of will, whether it is conscious or not. Whenever we are acting from will we cannot surrender

- we cannot let go.

And so our task is to move into a state of acceptance of whatever is real and alive in this moment, whether it be fear or anger or grief. We do not deny it or try to change it, but simply become aware of it, become present to it. We accept whatever is happening as perfect. There is no need to find fault with anything that is happening with us. There is no cause for any belief that we are doing something wrong, or failing, or somehow we are inadequate. Where we are in this moment is perfect. It couldn't be any other way.

We turn our awareness inward. We feel our bodies and become present to what is real in this moment. We observe without judgment how we are holding ourselves; and where there is tension, discomfort or pain. We do not judge it. As we bring understanding and acceptance, we are bringing our knowledge of the truth - that we are born into this life on a journey, a journey of growth, learning and expansion.

From the start, we never intended to be perfect if we understand *perfect* to mean *completely free.* If you understand the nature of life, you understand that perfection exists in every moment; it is complete and total. Harmony and order are the only possibilities. Your journey to this point in your life has been an endless stream of miracles, whether you have recognized them or not: you are alive, you are awake, you are conscious, and all of your needs are met in every moment.

There is no model for who you should be in this moment other than exactly what you are. You are unfolding in a unique and divine way. No one has ever been like you or ever will be. No one has any right to say you should be different in any way. Your unique being fills a very specific need in the evolution of life. Your part to play is uniquely your own and is not like anyone else's. There is no way to compare yourself to anyone. There is no standard to judge yourself by. There is nothing of the sort. All you can do is express more and more freely that which is you, which originates in God, that which is the joyful pouring forth of Spirit through you – that which always has been, always will be.

Understand this about your life: the trauma you look back on now, which colors your trust in God, was not judged by you in the way that you see it now. You have responded to it and carried on. You did not let it stop you. The suffering you believed was caused by that trauma was not; the suffering was caused by forgetting who you were. The trauma was caused by not accepting yourself exactly as you are right now. The suffering was directly a result of believing that you should somehow be different. Nothing is wrong with you. Nothing has gone wrong in your life. Nothing should be better. Everything you want and need exists right now within you. Your physical life is an expression of your consciousness. Your consciousness is an expression of God. There is nothing you lack, that you are missing or that is not good enough about you.

In this moment allow yourself to know the truth of your own divine nature - a nature that has been perfect and always will be perfect and is perfect right now. You are not more powerful than God. You do not have the ability to create the truth outside of God. There is no power other than God. Any belief that somehow you are not adequate, you are a failure, you are wrong or not good enough is false pride. False pride is believing that you, on your own, are a creative being that exists separately from God. This is impossible. It is an illusion, a hallucination.

When we are not connected with reality we hallucinate - we don't know the truth of ourselves and live in a false world. When we don't accept our feelings of rage, anger, terror, fear or grief, we are not accepting reality. When we judge those feelings, we are not accepting reality. Allow yourself to be who you are, where you are right now. Do nothing but accept. And from accepting you can move to allowing, saying *yes* to the presence of God within you, allowing the experience of your own divine nature to flood your awareness, to fill your consciousness, to truly become who you are.

Remember this: despite all the objections from your ego, you cannot possibly be anything but an expression of God, expressing perfectly in this moment. Any idea or concept that you are anything else is a hallucination.

38. FROM BELIEF IN EGO TO TRUST IN GOD

It is important to understand the process of how we came to believe and to have faith in our ego. On a physical level, the trauma of our past when we were vulnerable and dependent led us to block or shut down the flow of energy in our bodies. What we learned from the trauma and the overwhelming circumstances was that certain expressions of our life force were not welcome or were dangerous to our survival. With either conscious or unconscious control we closed off energetic pathways to prevent their expression.

In a natural relaxed state of being there is energetic flow throughout our body and our responses to situations are based on the information we get from our body. But we learned we could not trust this natural source of information; we had to be in control in some other way. And so we closed down that system to some degree, and began to respond to situations by analyzing them. To whatever degree we closed down those pathways, we closed down our ability to respond to life in the most life-enhancing and health-giving ways. Instead we learned to respond in ways that would keep us from being humiliated, rejected, abandoned or in some way harmed.

The fact is, we didn't stop our body from responding; we only stopped our conscious awareness of these responses. Our body continued to respond but the mind, (the ego), exerted control over the body, preventing a natural system of responses. So, in effect, what has happened is that we have become afraid of the life force within us. We are afraid to express it, afraid to surrender to it, afraid to trust it. We only trust our mind, our analysis, our knowledge. We trust history. We believe that what happened in the past will happen again. We believe that life is a linear process that is following an inevitable chain of events. We believe that we must know and control all the events in our life. We believe in our ego. We have faith in it.

It's not unusual for us to find that our body is a source of disappointment or failure, even disgust or abhorrence. We are ashamed of it when, in fact, it is the instrument of God. Our body is the means of reflecting God's expression back to God so that God sees itself through our physical experience. God has no capacity to judge, no will to change. God has only to express.

We often see our body as a handicap, some kind of impediment to fulfilling our life. In fact, there would be nothing to think that thought without a body. Our biggest impediment to fulfillment and a satisfying life is our belief that somehow there is someone in charge other than God, that the ego is real and can be trusted. What we have learned is that when we feel certain feelings in our body there is something wrong. Then our ego becomes more and more controlling, trying to analyze the problem.

If we feel fear we think there is something wrong. If we feel anger we think there is something wrong - that somehow we are failing, we are in danger, something terrible is going to happen, we are going to make a mistake, or we are going to make a mess. For many of us the one thing we cannot stand is to make a mess. It activates every fear particle in our being to have that degree of being out-of-control. We would sacrifice our own happiness to prevent a mess.

If only we could see in that moment the impossibility of getting something wrong, of making a mistake, the impossibility of the illusion that we are in control. If only we could see that when we are most compelled to make decisions that could lead to disaster we are being guided most directly with the hand of God which can only guide us to expansion and growth, to more good. It cannot guide us to danger, to harm, to smallness – only to good.

If we could only see that when what lies before us seems more frightening and overwhelming than anything we have done, it is instead, exactly what we are supposed to be doing, and the hand of God is right with us in every moment. The only thing causing our discomfort is lack of trust.

We are not two-year-olds who have failed our potty training. We are not three-year-olds who have had our sexual love rejected. We are God at work. Moving from belief in the ego to faith in God is a process that needs to be undertaken over and over again. But there cannot be any process with a bigger payoff. We have known miracles, we have known magic, we have known the power of oneness, beauty, truth, the magnificence of love, the joy of creativity. We know that all this is true.

In the mind of God there has never been any question of your perfection. Whether you experience that or not, it is still true. There is nowhere that you are going except right here, right now. Your life is truly like a dream. Your habit is to create a nightmare. Now you can create a dream.

39. TRAPPED IN OUR BODIES

Many of us feel trapped in our body. The body can be a source of pain and discomfort and we believe we exist separate from it, that we aren't really part of it and it is like an unfriendly companion we are stuck with. To many of us, it seems our body has betrayed us. We feel it has led to nothing but trouble. It appeared to be the source of our parents' disapproval or other damaging feelings. And we came to think of ourselves as the person who lives in our head either trying to control our body or trying to disassociate from it.

If we identify with any of these feelings, then we know we are logged into a belief in separation - our ego has become our identity and we have lost our sense of connection and truth. Although it is true that we are not our body, it is also true that we are not our ego identity. Rather we are the source of our body; we are the cause. We are not victims of the pain and discomfort in our body; we are the source of the pain and discomfort.

Without our body we would have no way to know who we are.

It is through our human physical bodies that we can reflect on our true nature. It is through the deep, energetic pathway that connects us all with everything else that we become self-aware, that we can experience our own infinite nature.

We sit here now in this moment in time and we have a conscious mind that thinks, reflects, repeats belief systems habitually and makes judgments. Most of the time it is so preoccupied with what is wrong or what is going to be wrong, that there is no room for anything else. It is nearly impossible for us to keep true perspective on ourselves and our life.

But now we see that we do observe that mind. We can see that it is true that even now, our mind is calling our attention to its agenda. Even in this moment, it wants us to worry, to plan, to go over and over things, to judge. Even now, it is telling us that there is something wrong, there is something bad. Even if we just have a headache it's got plenty to say about that.

To become truly present we have to accept that we are the pain. The pain is not being done to us. We are the pain. We are the cause. We are not a victim. The victim that suffers from the headache is just a figment of our imagination, a powerful and habitual one, one we believe in and put our faith in. However, it's not real.

What is real is that in this moment we are creating our body and we are holding on in certain ways, we are not letting go and we are not surrendering. And so we experience discomfort and a sense of separation. We do not judge this; we must not judge. We accept it and understand that we are the cause. Our consciousness is the source of our world.

The more we accept *what is* right now as a reflection of our consciousness, the more we can surrender and let go. The more we become present, absolutely present, to *what is,* the more we can let go. When we begin to understand that we are the source, then we begin to affirm the truth and align ourselves with the truth of who we are. We begin to acknowledge that there is only one power. We begin to feel that we are not separate from that power. We see that power as a power for good and contains no evil or no wrong. There is no power other than the one universal, loving spirit. There is no power in our body that can overcome the power of God. There is no power in the world that can overcome the power of God. There is no other power. Everything emerges from this one source, is contained within it, is filled with it and exists within it.

There is within you right now a capacity for peace, a capacity for stillness, a capacity for feeling perfect health, a capacity for a healing presence that restores everything to perfection in this moment. That is what's true about you. That is what lives within you right now, right here.

Surrender now. Say *yes* to peace. Say *yes* to God. Be willing to give up your control. Be willing to say *yes.* Allow yourself to surrender to your own divine nature. Allow it to happen now. You can stop fighting now. You can stop swimming upstream. You can stop doing it all on your own.

If you took the time, everywhere you looked you would see signs that God is guiding you with wisdom and love. If you took the time to acknowledge what a miracle your life is, you would see the powerful gifts you have been given, the effortless journeys, the transitions, the growth you have made. Stop fighting now. Let go.

40. LOVE IS THE ONLY POWER

As we have discussed previously, the most important skill for you to master is moving from survival to creativity. You are by now well aware of how easily survival mode takes over, how easy it is to begin to see limitation, lack, danger, threats, and how quickly we begin to engage with them to try to change them, try to fix them, while staying in survival mode. All we can do in survival mode is manipulate and try to control the world, tinkering in the world of secondary cause, moving things about, shifting the order of things without achieving any real change or growth.

To achieve what we really deeply want to achieve, what our soul wants to achieve, what will bring satisfaction and peace, we must be in creative mode. We must see and know the truth of every situation, of every person, of ourselves. We must act from that seeing and knowing. Only then do we make progress in letting go of our old beliefs, our old limitations, and our old habits. So we constantly remind ourselves that we are not here to fix the world by tinkering with it, by adjusting it, by fixing it. We are here to add to the world our own unique gifts and creative input. We are here to bring our own way of expressing the divine in action. We are here to be who we truly are, not to do what we think is best.

And so we tirelessly remind ourselves that when we are experiencing judgment, problems, things being wrong, limitation and lack, it is time for us to stop and realign ourselves with the truth. To do this requires letting go of our fear, our worry, our doubt, our struggle – all the forces that create a comfortable state of mind, one which we are happy to act in and to hold onto, because it is so comfortable. There is a way that it is habitually comfortable, even though it frustrates us and causes great discomfort. We must be willing to stop and realign ourselves in that moment.

We no longer have viable excuses. We no longer can claim that we didn't know. We are well aware of the truth. God is or God isn't. We trust or we don't. We surrender or we don't. We let go or we don't.

Now we come to the moment when it is necessary to realign ourselves. There is resistance. There is always resistance. We would not be in survival mode if there was not resistance. We don't judge the resistance. We observe it. We notice it. We allow it. We accept it. We remember that resistance is a natural phenomenon, a natural response. In this moment right now it is completely expected that we would have resistance. We do not fight it. We accept it and we turn our attention back to the truth, back to the knowledge that there is one power and one power only and that we exist within this power. There is nothing outside of this power.

There is no part of us that is separate. There is no part of us that is other than this power. Every single aspect of our being is an aspect of this power for good – even our resistance. Everything about us is an expression of this divine power expressing as us in our own unique and evolving way. Not one of us was born with the capacity that we are developing right now: to know that we are not God and to know that we are. No one was born perfect and then ruined. That is an illusion. We are born as physical humans and through struggles and growth we evolve an awareness of our infinite nature - a self-awareness - that was impossible without the struggle. Everything in our life has been designed to bring us to a deep self-awareness of our infinite nature.

We reaffirm and realign ourselves with the truth of our own divine path, divine order, divine harmony that operates in every way in every aspect of our lives. And we reaffirm that anything that seems other than this is merely a projection of our mind, an illusion created by our imagination - a misuse of our imagination.

Allow yourself to let go. Allow yourself to surrender. Allow yourself to remember to trust in God, to have faith in the one power, to remember that anything that doesn't look like love is not real.

Love is the only power. Take this in at the deepest level and understand the importance of this statement. Love is the only power. There is nothing else.

41. THE SWEET SURRENDER

The purpose of this meditation is to allow you to become present, to let go of control and surrender your resistance so that you can have a pure experience of your true self, so you can experience the sweetness and lightness of truth, of being fully present and fully aware. Remember that the experience of peace and freedom is always available to you, and that peace and freedom is alive and present within you in every moment. When it is your intention to return to this experience and you hold fast to the knowledge and awareness of its existence, it is inevitable that you will let go and surrender. But you must also hold the intention of accepting your resistance, acknowledging but not resisting it. You are moving away from doing and into being, simply being. You are not going to manipulate anything. You are not going to fix or improve anything. Nothing is broken - nothing is working incorrectly. Everything is proceeding perfectly with or without your acceptance.

We easily are led to believe that when we are not surrendered, we are creating problems for ourselves and that life is not proceeding perfectly. The truth is that life is proceeding perfectly in every moment. There is no other way for it to proceed. Our only challenge is whether to accept "what is" in the moment or not, to become present or not, to remember the truth or not. Holding the intention of accepting, becoming present, surrendering our resistance, and letting go of control, we turn our attention within and are no longer interested in the chatter of our ego. We direct our awareness, we focus on our inner experience and become aware of our body, become aware of our breathing, become aware of all our inner sensations without judging or analyzing them. We do not think about it; we observe it. We are just looking; we look at it with our awareness. As we let our awareness grow stronger in its focus on our inner world, we remember and affirm the truth. While our awareness is focused on observing our sensations, we repeat in our minds the following:

I know that there is only one power. I know that within me now this power is alive and present. I know that I can let go and surrender to this presence. I accept my resistance, I am aware of it. I know it is there. I do not judge it; I simply observe it. I treat myself with compassion and understanding. I understand the resistance is a natural phenomenon. I am aware of the presence of a living energy within me. I become more and more focused in my awareness. I consciously choose to let go of control in this moment. I am willing to trust in God. I am willing to open and allow. I am aware of the presence of God within me. I remember now that I can let go, I can surrender. I remember the feeling of peace. In every moment now I can let go more deeply. In every moment now, the feeling of peace grows stronger. I remember that I am an expression of a beautiful, divine power. I remember that this divine power is always within me. I let go and surrender to this power. I let go and surrender to the peace within me. I willingly choose to surrender to the power within me. I choose to trust and let go. The feeling of presence within me grows stronger. I trust and open. I let go of control. I remember the sweet feeling of letting go and opening, the joy of trusting. I can truly relax and know I am safe. I accept and acknowledge my resistance and let it go, for I know the joy of release. Now I continue to open, to allow the surrender. I release my resistance.

42. PERSISTENT BLOCKS

In our daily lives there are things we want to obtain, goals we want to accomplish, experiences we want to have, relationships we desire and long for. Yet, there are times when we feel blocked in attaining these ends; it seems that we make no progress or we see glimmers of progress, but then it seems we are back to where we were before. It's not hard to understand how we might feel despair and hopelessness even though we seem to be doing everything we can to make changes.

These particular blocks, these persistent areas where we seem to make no progress, are truly the frontiers of our spiritual growth. They are the treasures of our journey. They hold the key to the storeroom where the secrets we long to know are held: how to find true peace, how to create a meaningful and satisfying life abundant with joy and bliss. These stubborn areas in our life are a blessing when we recognize them. We are lucky to identify the frontier. So we must come to understand the dynamics of this seeming block in our flow.

Every one of us made a decision to turn away from our true nature and develop a strategy for surviving and fitting in. Every one of us came up with a completely unique solution to the overwhelming trauma of our childhoods. There is a story about us that explains our decision, that describes our solution, that justifies our current situation. There is always some sort of victimization in that story. There is always the good and the bad, the right and the wrong.

As we progress on our path, our spiritual journey we become conscious of the beliefs that have colored our view, and we begin to piece together the survival strategies behind parts of the story. We begin to see the self-protective decisions we made; we begin to understand that we did indeed turn away from God - turn away from our own natural guidance. We turned our attention to the way of being that would keep us safe and allow us to escape with as little pain as possible.

But to turn completely to the world of the mind, the intellect, is rarely satisfying or fulfilling. Our heart longs for expression. Our soul calls us to express and connect with our true nature. And so, we find ways in our life to connect with beauty and truth, but we see them as secondary to staying safe - to avoiding pain. The need for control still dominates. This is the ego's solution to the painful loss of connection with our self.

In time we begin to see the ways that we really have sidelined our true self, and we become aware of our justification for doing this. We begin to see the themes that recur in our life and we begin to understand that there is a powerful justification within us at an unconscious level for keeping some degree of control in our life. But, by now, we have learned that to truly surrender and trust is the only way to experience what we want.

Even though we now know this to be true, unconsciously we still believe it not to be true in every area of our life. Unconsciously, we are saying, *there is a part of me that I need to control. There is a part of me that is somehow less than perfect. Despite all I believe and know about my true nature, that is not true about my defect. There is an area in my life where I am undeserving and unworthy, and I must be in control.*

As we become conscious and aware of these persistent blocks, what we know is that they protect us from deep pain. The agreement we made with ourselves, completely unconsciously, was to sacrifice our freedom to avoid the pain. When the agreement was made, the pain was overwhelming and we had no way to know that we wouldn't die as a direct result of it.

Now we are stronger. We know that we are not so vulnerable and dependent and that we are not alone. To take the risk and face the pain now does not put us at risk of dying (although we must accept our own death: the death of our story, our identity, our justification). Now we can see that the cause of these persistent blocks in our life was the exchange we made for avoiding the pain. There is no shame or judgment in that agreement. Everything in our being told us that it was the only way for us to survive. No one can criticize that decision.

As we know now from the previous discussion, the way forward to freedom and healing is compassion, love and acceptance of our decision and our agreement and acknowledgment of the deep loss and pain, giving comfort and nurture. These are the ways forward. Previously, our response to our pain was to do what we were taught and we became the perpetrators of our own pain and loss. Now, we are maturing into being capable of unconditionally loving ourselves, accepting ourselves, nurturing, comforting, and bringing compassion and love to all of our resistance. This is who we are becoming.

43. A SIMPLE YES

It is easy to forget that the presence of God within us is not a heavy energy. It is not a serious energy. It is not judgmental, rewarding or punishing. It is not controlling. It is not withholding. It is never disappointed, let down or frustrated. It is incapable of seeing imperfection, flaws, inadequacy, or failure. None of that exists in the energy that is love. Love is the very basis of our being, so there is no need for effort or trying hard. There is no work ethic.

We often carry out our lives as if we are trying to please someone, to make someone happy, to be good enough, to be accepted. Or we set ourselves aside, apart, separate and tell ourselves that we don't care. The truth is that within each one of us is a deep longing for connection, a deep longing for love, for the experience of complete acceptance of who we are, complete recognition of who we are. This longing has been buried, denied, suppressed, repressed and turned in to all kinds of desires, habits and addictions.

But the undeniable truth is that our spirit is alive and present. It continues to seek expression as our authentic selves. The call of our soul urges us to become freer - to let go of our restrictions and limits. Our spirit is unquenchable. It is not impatient. It is not forceful. It is simply present, expressing exactly as you are. Spirit is potential. It is possibilities and it is infinite in its power.

There is nothing that needs to be done to make yourself good enough. There is no need to work hard at improving yourself. There is nothing you can add to yourself. It is quite the opposite. You are letting go of the layers of beliefs, ideas and concepts. You are releasing the past. You are relaxing into your true self. There is nothing to do, there is only to stop doing.

The presence of God is alive within you in every moment. In this moment there is nothing wrong. There is nothing that needs to be done to fix anything. Everything you need, everything you are looking for, everything you desire is here right now. The infinite nature of spirit is alive within you. Infinite means that everything that has existed or will exist is within you now. You cannot have a part of infinity. There is only the whole. You cannot be separate from infinity. There is no way to be outside of it. You cannot be anything other. You can think you are. You can believe you are. But you cannot be separate. This is the truth about you right now. This is the truth about you in every moment. There is nothing you can do to change your infinite nature.

There is nothing you can do to separate yourself from God. There is no part of you that is not God - that is not love. There is no part of you that is not good enough - no part of you that is bad. If you could accept this truth, you would be transformed.

If you are resistant, you will suffer. If you say *yes* to the knowledge of your own divine nature, if you allow it to be true, if you stop insisting on limitation, if you will accept that even your resistance is the love of God at work, then you can be transformed. Then your heart can open and you can experience the love of God alive within you.

Can you stop and say *yes* to all that is real in this moment? Can you say *yes* to whatever is alive within you? Can you accept yourself just as you are in this moment? Can you affirm that only love exists in this moment, that whatever is alive within you in this moment is created by love? We have no power to do anything on our own. There is only one power.

To surrender, to become the truth, we must take the leap of trusting and letting go. We must release our grip. The presence of God within us is a powerful healing presence knowing exactly what we need if we will surrender to it, if we will say *yes* to our own spirit, if we will give up our control, our determination that we are alone. It is all here right now expressing as who we are right in this moment.

God has not made any mistakes. Divine order and perfect harmony are always the law. We have not reached this point by accident or luck. There is no argument against your perfection. Resistance is not a failure. Love is never withheld, is never absent. To surrender now is your choice - a simple *yes.*

44. A FOCUS FOR MEDITATION

There is one key ability we all need to develop on our spiritual path that will aid us in surrendering and letting go. It's the ability to turn our focus from our egoic mind - from our thoughts, beliefs and identity - and to know that we are something other than that with which we are strongly identified. We begin to know that thoughts, ideas and beliefs are just transient forms of energy and are not a coherent being or power.

Many of us have been unaware that there is anything else to experience besides our identity. In every moment the ego is active and asserts itself into our awareness. Most of the time we believe what it says: there are problems, there's something wrong, there is something bad, or there are threats. Right now, in this moment, our ego is asserting its control so that we will not surrender. Its activity is causing us discomfort, tension, anxiety, and fear. We must learn to observe these processes of the ego, to accept them, and to know they are not us. The ego is fully capable of keeping us distracted for a full meditation period. But we are fully capable of turning the focus of our awareness inward; in other words, we can choose in this moment what to pay attention to.

The ego loses its power whenever our attention is not on it. To move our attention from the ego, we simply observe our breath consistently and totally. We expand our awareness beyond the limits of the ego. If we pay total attention to any part of our body and focus totally on that, we can begin to become still.

As we become more and more focused, our awareness expands so that we sense our entire body. When this happens we feel areas that might be tense, sore, or uncomfortable. We can sense our overall state of relaxation. We do not have to judge or think about it, we are just noticing; we allow our awareness to perceive our entire body. As we observe our state of relaxation, we can allow ourselves to relax even more and we can allow ourselves to let go of holding. We know in this moment that we are safe and there is nothing to watch out for.

We can use the power of our imagination to assist us in letting go. We can imagine the feeling of being perfectly relaxed. Now imagine what it feels like to be completely relaxed. Feel that feeling of simply letting go. In this moment there is nothing to be done, nothing to do except relax. There is no time pressure, no schedule, no jobs or tasks. Just imagine feeling total peace and relaxation. There is no conflict, no drama, nothing to fear. Imagine that feeling. Imagine that as you sit here in this moment, your body is becoming softer and relaxed even more. Imagine the feeing of opening. As your body softens, it opens. The difference between you and the air around you is becoming less defined. You are becoming soft, open, and fuzzy around the edges.

Now imagine there is a light inside you, an energy, a warmth. Imagine it spreading through you, bringing peace and stillness - a feeling that everything is fine. You can relax now. Let this light, this energy, move through you, and diffuse out through you. Only pay attention to the light.

Now imagine the feeling of your heart opening. Feel love washing through you - a feeling of tenderness and compassion. Imagine that feeling. Now imagine a loving presence alive within you - a love that you long for. Become aware of your longing to surrender to this presence within you, your longing to be engulfed in love.

45. EVERYTHING IS ENERGY

It is useful to remember that everything, including this physical world, is really just energy. There is nothing that is permanent or solid; even that which seems dense and unchanging is just energy. This is particularly important to remember about our bodies and what we perceive as ourselves. It is tempting to believe that these bodies are solid, unchanging, and fixed the way they are in this moment. But, in reality, our bodies are just energy responding to other energetic forces, creating patterns of vibration which arise in our consciousness as our perception of matter.

But there is no matter. Everything is vibration and energy. It is simply our mind that interprets energy as different forms of matter. The pattern of energy and vibrations gives form to our physical body as a direct manifestation of our consciousness. Any change in our consciousness is reflected immediately in the physical world. The change may be too subtle to recognize right away, but it is there nonetheless.

If we only knew, if we only truly believed and comprehended

that consciousness is all there is, that every thought we think has an effect, that every belief creates a pattern, a vibration, the power at our disposal would be magnificent. The truth is that we use that power in every moment, but our view of what is possible is so limited, so rigid, that we barely experience any change in the world.

Our temptation to tinker with the world and try to repair it distracts us constantly from our true ability to create change. Our lack of trust in the power of God within us constantly forces us to waste action. There is no escaping the truth, the truth that we are creating our lives in this moment according to the limits we have placed on, what is in fact, unlimited power. We are creating our lives according to what we imagine is impossible, what we imagine is good, what we imagine is right; we use our imagination to shape the world in every moment.

We feel it is difficult to know our unconscious beliefs. We don't understand why we are creating a world that doesn't seem to fit our needs or wants. The simple answer is that we don't believe that we can do any different. What we are experiencing in the world at the moment is what we believe is the best that we can do. For some reason we are not surprised at how much we limit ourselves.

The idea of unlimited power to create daunts us or even frightens us. We turn away. We prefer the comfort of our limited vision. We prefer to make small adjustments here and there to keep it from getting too uncomfortable. We do not dare to think of creating magnificence. We do not dare to have a huge vision. We do not dare to imagine unlimited possibilities.

We are like a child presented with a blank sheet of paper and a set of crayons who is so daunted by the big space that they can only draw in one corner. The possibility of making a mistake or a mess is too frightening to allow the use of the whole paper. We seem to think that we only get one chance, and that when we make a mess we can't undo it. We really don't understand unlimited possibility. We really don't believe in it. We are so afraid of making a mistake.

And yet, what is true is that we are just energy. Energy can change in a moment. Everything can be transformed in one moment. The real world is the world of love, the world of creativity, of beauty, of harmony and order. That is what is real. That is what is alive within us seeking expression. The real world knows nothing of mistakes, messes, wrong or bad. There is no such thing. The real world is energy seeking to flow, to be free, to expand. It is the vibration of music seeking harmony.

No one and nothing is served by our limited vision, by our keeping things small, by our insistence that we must do things right, that we cannot take the chance of failing. There is nothing but energy, vibration. Your consciousness emerges from the one source. You are the source expressing through love. There is nothing impure or imperfect about you. You arise from perfection. The vibration and energy of the power of love is who you are. There is no requirement for you to be good, to be right, to not fail, to fit in. There is no requirement of you whatsoever. There is no judgment, no standard to meet. You will not be evaluated.

Within you right now is all the power of the one divine source, the loving vibration that creates everything. Everything you experience is based on your expectation – everything. Know

now that you are one with God. God is present in everything. Your life is God's life and God's life is your life. You will be free of resistance for resistance is not real. Only love is real.

46. OVERCOMING VICTIMIZATION

It's not unusual for us to find ourselves feeling victimized - powerless in relation to something in our lives, whether its effect is inside of us or outside of us. We come to believe that we are being negatively affected by an external power, that we are being treated unfairly, that we are sick, or impacted in any number of ways that lead us to believe something or someone has power over us.

This belief is so structured into most cultures that when anything appears to go wrong in our lives, it is almost automatic to blame a power outside of ourselves - to see ourselves as victims. It has become our custom to demand that the world change to suit us, because we firmly believe that our quality of life is dependent on forces outside of us.

And yet, everything that we know about universal truth shows that there is no power outside of us; there is only the power within us. This state of victimization develops when the ego is in charge. The ego has captivated our focus, demanding that we look at how wrong things are, how bad things are, and how much we must be on guard and on alert for danger. And, at this point, there is no chance of peace or freedom. Our energy system is then mobilized for survival. Our focus is captured by the world of secondary cause and effect. We begin to desperately make changes in this world to relieve the feeling of victimization, of being powerless.

It is worth noting that there are times when it is appropriate to take measures. If we have a sickness that is causing us sorrow and we cannot stop it simply by returning to what is true, it may be helpful to take other steps as well. But we must be conscious that when we do this we are choosing to believe in a secondary power, even though we know that there is no such thing. Sometimes our level of awareness and consciousness is not up to the job of overcoming our beliefs in secondary powers. Our first priority then is to acknowledge that and go on to develop and deepen our spiritual practice – not to continue to find ways of making adjustments in the world of secondary causes, though that may be necessary for a short time.

We need to acknowledge that there are subconscious beliefs and ideas in our energetic system that we have not released. Acknowledging this is an important step in taking responsibility on our spiritual journey - indeed, it is the main step towards overcoming our feelings of victimization. We are taking a big step when we acknowledge that we are responsible for creating circumstances and situations in our life. When we do this we have moved closer to the truth. From there we can pray. We can ask for answers. We can seek guidance. We can turn to the true source of our life and remember who we are.

We do not always have to know why we are attracting or

creating certain effects in our lives. What needs to be revealed will be revealed. But we do need to take responsibility for these effects because there is no question that we are creating our lives right now. Our goal is to return to what is true in this moment, to become present to what is real, to accept and recognize the truth. The truth is that all the world of secondary effects and causes, all the physical world, all that we experience, is simply the out-picturing of consciousness. Just like a picture on a movie screen - simply light - there is no physical reality to what you are seeing. It is simply energy.

So we acknowledge and recognize that our consciousness creates this world through the filter of our unconscious beliefs and ideas and what we experience as a result is a mirror of what we expect. We recognize as well that all of that can change in an instant. When we recognize our role in creating what we see, we take responsibility for creating what we want. What we do not always understand is that we are guided. Our pathway is always unfolding toward greater consciousness and awareness toward waking up. Our soul never abandons its quest for us to fully realize who we are.

Even when our resistance seems highest and our ability to surrender seems non-existent, we are still on the path. There is something we are revealing and we will get insight and healing if we trust. If only we can remember to trust. If only we can remember that love is all there is, that nothing happens without love, that there is no other power but love. If we can keep this in mind, we will release our struggle and our suffering and we will be free.

So, we can let go. We can surrender knowing that we are always in the presence of God, guided by love, and that we are already whole and complete. It is only a matter of time before we will allow ourselves to experience the truth.

47. DISTRACTING OURSELVES FROM FEAR

You have a list of things in your life that aren't right. You carry this list around in your head, planning to work hard to correct these problems, whatever your deficiencies may be. They may be aspects of your physical body, aspects of your thinking, or they may be things that you are doing or not doing that need to be changed. In this moment right now is there something that's not right - something that needs to change, be fixed, or something that needs to be improved? Is there something that's holding your attention with its wrongness so that your energy and attention is focused on correcting this problem, engaging with it, giving it life?

When you reflect on it, has that list of problems continued to have very similar issues on it for a long time? Does it seem like you are always trying to correct or fix the same kind of problem? Is that where you place your energy, your thought, your activity, your focus?

Many of us distract ourselves from fears by placing our focus and energy on the outside world. The outside world includes our body, our physical health, physical symptoms, and our physical feelings. In this moment, what is preventing you from stopping and paying attention to what is inside you, instead of what is outside of you? It may seem like it is an issue that needs attention - a symptom, pain or discomfort in your body. It may seem like there are a hundred things to stop you. None of those things have any power - so how can they stop you?

You can't be a victim to them. It's impossible. At some level, some area of your consciousness is choosing to energize the resistance or the distraction, and choosing to avoid facing the fear. There is nothing bad about this. It is not shameful, weak or anything. It simply is. Our goal is to become conscious of how we distract ourselves when we have forgotten who we are. Our goal is to return to the truth. Very few of us are currently experiencing a true survival emergency, but we act as if we are.

What is your intention in this moment? Is it to remember the truth? Or is it to pay attention to the resistance? You can't do both. Resistance seems real; it seems powerful. It seems like it has the ability to control us, to stop us from remembering who we are. Resistance seems like it can stop us from letting go - stop us from surrendering. In reality, resistance is simply a choice we are making. It may be more or less conscious but it is a choice.

When we remember that we have choices, and when we acknowledge that, we move closer to letting go. When we see that we are choosing to avoid our fear of surrender - our fear of loss of control - we begin to recover our authentic self. When we say that our resistance is stopping us, we are not authentic – we are victims. When we say, *I am afraid to let go*, we are speaking the truth. Whether we feel the fear or not, whether we really understand it or not, it is there. It is the only reason for resistance. There is no other reason.

So our journey is not to constantly engage with resistance, but to acknowledge the fear. Our journey is to become conscious of the choice we are making and decide whether that is the choice we want to make, or will we choose to surrender despite the fear. Will we choose to remember the truth? Will we choose to allow ourselves to open to what is already alive within us? Are we willing to move our attention away from our resistance onto what is truly alive within us?

When we discover that fear is active, can we recover compassion and kindness, acceptance and forgiveness? Can we begin right now to nurture and cultivate feelings of warmth and love for ourselves just as we are? Can we accept that whatever we are thinking or feeling, there is a perfection or order about our lives right now? Can we accept that there is an evolving and an unfolding of our consciousness that is not a linear process? Can we accept that there are peaks and valley and seemingly wrong turns?

When we view our lives through the filter of the conditioned human mind, it is as if we are trying to understand a beautiful woven fabric by looking at one thread. If we thought that we had to take that one thread and make a beautiful fabric, we would be overwhelmed and frustrated. And yet, that's what we do. We think that we are somehow separate from the big picture. We think there is something special about us, something different, we can be separate, and we can stand outside of God and be imperfect.

The truth is that the big picture is complete within us but we are afraid of it. We are afraid of our ability to make people uncomfortable. We are afraid we might make people dislike us. We are afraid to shine brightly. We insist that we are in control - that we can determine who sees what, who feels what, who has what response. We do not trust ourselves to be loving and kind. We are forever trying to subdue the monster within us.

This is why when we become conscious of our fear, we must take responsibility for our choice to pay attention to the distractions and our resistance, rather than acknowledging the fear and surrendering. The only appropriate response to this fear is compassion and kindness, understanding and acceptance. Otherwise we become our own harsh judge.

Now, in this moment, we make the choice to allow ourselves to open and feel the resistance. We continue to choose to allow. The resistance is not in charge – it's not a power. It is a fantasy of fear and it will dissolve when you see it for what it is. Continue to choose to open to what is really true, to what is always true, to what is infinite and giving us life in this moment.

48. AWARENESS IS LIKE A VACUUM

There is a quality of consciousness called awareness and every waking moment our awareness is filled with something. In this moment, what are you aware of? Are you paying attention to your thoughts? Are you listening to the sounds around you? Are you feeling sensations in your body? Most of the time, for most of us, our awareness is full of thoughts: worrying, anxiety, trying to solve problems, planning, thinking ahead. Sometimes it is directed at things that entertain us. Sometimes it is directed at things that distract us.

The most important aspect of awareness is that we direct it. We choose what we are aware of, whether consciously or unconsciously. Right now you can shift your awareness from the sound of the rain to feeling your breath moving in and out, or to a feeling in your head or your neck. You choose what to pay attention to. If I say, *listen to the rain*, that is what you become aware of. If I say, *feel your body in contact with the floor*, you can feel those parts of you that are touching the floor right now.

Awareness is like a vacuum - it seeks to be filled. Awareness does not discern or judge. It takes what it is aware of as reality, as truth. It makes no decisions. It is simply aware. If we sit and process ideas of lack and limitation, awareness accepts that lack and limitation are real. If we process ideas of impending disaster, awareness believes that disaster is impending. If we keep our focus and attention on the world around us, awareness accepts that as reality.

Consciousness creates the world based on our awareness. For many of us, what we choose to be aware of is largely an unconscious process. Awareness will always seek to be filled, so if we are not consciously choosing, we will be unconsciously choosing. The default of unconscious choice is to be distracted – distracted from discomfort, from uncomfortable realizations. Awareness does not seek a challenging path; it seeks an easy one.

In contrast, the process of becoming awake and conscious means recognizing uncomfortable truths. We consider how we have not loved, accepted, or forgiven ourselves and others. We review painful moments that we have experienced and not let go of, and we look at parts of ourselves that we have denied and repressed. Although becoming awake is not always a comfortable experience, it is always rewarding. It always leads to growth and expansion.

If we are not choosing to be conscious and aware, our default will be distraction. In every waking moment throughout the day we can choose to be aware of truth or involved with the distraction in front of us.

The nature of a spiritual journey is to develop greater and more permanent awareness of who we truly are, to be conscious of what we are choosing, and to recognize our ability to choose in any given moment. For most of us, turning our awareness away from distraction, and turning inward to what is alive within us, leads us to an awareness of resistance and fear. This is why we avoid it. Our resistance and fear makes us feel powerless and victimized. To a large degree we believe the resistance and fear are powers. We believe that they are real. In reality, they are only distractions.

In this moment, turn your awareness to what is alive within you, whatever it is. Experience yourself. Do not be distracted by the physical world - the world of your thoughts. Just experience yourself. That means to pay attention to what you perceive within you. We use the term *within* to signify turning our awareness away from the world of the five senses and onto our perception of ourselves – turning to our inner experience. This is when we are most likely to be distracted by thoughts and resistance. But there is a world of experience alive within us waiting for us to awaken to it. There is a world within that ends distraction and makes us aware of what is real in this moment. In this context we become aware of holding, of fear, of tension.

The spirit of God is alive within us and we can perceive it, we can experience it. As we soften, relax and let go, we are more able to experience the spirit of God within us. If we are steadfast in keeping our awareness on what is real, we can perceive the spirit of God.

49. THE SPIRITUAL JOURNEY

It is common to believe that the spiritual journey is one of adding to yourself, making yourself better, learning new things, somehow improving yourself. There is some implication of hard work - the hard work of self-improvement. Some even refer to building spiritual muscle, and strengthening that muscle. There is an element of truth in this, but the real picture is substantially different.

Perhaps a reminder of that picture would help us remember how we have progressed. We know now that all the power, all the wisdom, all the love, exists in its totality in every moment and in every place. There is never anything missing from God. The spiritual journey is one of coming to express this fully - to free this infinite power within us. We are that. We are not trying to improve ourselves, rather, we are trying to stop ourselves from limiting the infinite power within us. The plain truth is that we expend tremendous amounts of energy trying to contain that power by trying to look normal, trying to fit in, and trying not to stand out. Our spiritual journey is to stop holding on - to release our grip on ourselves.

We are so afraid of what will happen if we let go. We wonder, *If we free that energy what will we do?* Most of us can't even imagine what would happen except that it would feel terrible and we are pretty certain it wouldn't be acceptable. We are certain that what lies within us is somehow tainted and corrupted, making us unacceptable, undesirable, and disapproved of. This is what we believe. This is why we hold on so tightly to this power within us. The irony is that we think we are seeking freedom, peace, and expansion in our lives, but really what we are looking for is a better way to control ourselves. We want to behave in a more spiritual way. We want to improve ourselves, and we imagine this is done by controlling our thoughts and beliefs. But we really don't want to free ourselves. We want to continue to train ourselves - to shape ourselves into something better. The one thing that we decided long ago and stuck to with remarkable tenacity is maintaining control of our self and our situation. We wear ourselves out trying to keep our power under control.

We shorten our lives. We wear out our bodies. We contract illnesses and diseases. And yet, some part of us won't let go. And there is nothing to say that we should let go. Do not misunderstand: it is perfectly natural that we have fear and ingrained habits. We couldn't be in any other position than we are right now. There is no shame in it. The reason we discuss this is to become conscious – not to make a judgment about where we are – but to understand where we are and see it from a bigger perspective.

Most of us have very limited awareness of how we hold on. Our belief is that if we do the right things, we will become better. And of course, there are things to do. But we must change the idea that there is anything missing and fully accept that we are indeed whole. That thought needs to be the very basis of our understanding of ourselves – our starting point. What we really struggle to understand is that our entire struggle to control our power has no effect whatsoever except in our own mind and our own experience. Struggling changes nothing. Our light is just as bright as it ever was. Our holding on simply consumes energy. It does not change anything and it increases the misery of our life experience. We can't change who we are. We never could. We never will be able to. Our personality, i.e., our identity and our ego, are a fantasy. In reality everything is energy. Our physical world is constructed by our brain interpreting energy. It is a primitive system. Your true self is as visible as any energy.

So we see now that we are involved in a pointless struggle: the nameless fear of death. And this is the crucial part of the journey. For the human has every right to fear death – it's built in – it is survival. And yet, there is more to us than our human selves. We will endure miserable circumstances to stay alive. But our soul knows there is no need to endure any misery. And so we are here now; we have chosen the spiritual path. We know, on some level, that there is more to us than our fear of death. But something is causing us to hold on, to fight, and to say *no* to letting go. By the very act of acknowledging our fear of death, we become bigger than it. We become the observer of it. We become a bigger power than our fear. But we must acknowledge it for what it is. We must see it. We must experience it. In this moment our soul yearns for freedom. Our heart yearns to open. We long for the freedom and peace of trusting.

And so let us come to accept in this moment that indeed, there is nothing missing – accept that nothing can be added to or subtracted from God. Our growing awareness of our infinite nature is calming the fear little by little. Trust is returning.

The peace and light are still there - are still here. Our beautiful nature has not been harmed. We are not damaged. The light is bright.

50. WE ARE POWERFUL CREATORS

We might wonder why we struggle so much with the idea of surrendering. Why is it so hard to let go and trust when the benefits of doing so seem so remarkable? Since most of us at one time have experienced the peace, the freedom, the joy, the love, the beauty - all the aspects of God that are available to us when we surrender - why is it so difficult to return to that experience?

To shed light on this conundrum, keep in mind that the physical world by itself has no power; it is an energetic system. Everything is energy and the physical world is just vibrations. We can now explore how we are deceived into believing that surrender might be dangerous.

At some point in our lifetime, perhaps very early in our childhood, every one of us had an experience that made us feel that our survival was threatened. In many cases our survival was threatened by the rejection, disapproval or anger of our parents on whom we were dependent. Before that, we had no experience of ourselves as different from the world; we did not perceive ourselves as separate. There was a harmony between ourselves and the world. We followed our natural impulses and did not deny them. Our needs were met. We did not want for anything. But then, whatever happened, whether it was deep trauma or some other form of rejection, the world became unfriendly. Danger was introduced; a threat to our survival appeared. We had to be on guard and alert. We had to control our natural impulses. We had to be careful to not offend whatever the nature of the threat. We had to fit in. Suddenly we experienced separation. We then had to negotiate our way in a hostile world and we were all alone to do it.

And this doesn't just happen on an individual basis. It is true on a cultural level too. This is the overriding belief of our culture. In our world there is much to support the idea that we are all alone, that there is no one to trust and that we must make our way through the world by ourselves. This is the world of the ego, the world where judgments, evaluations and analysis are made constantly. The way we were when we just followed our natural impulses and didn't see any difference between ourselves and the world became a distant memory. From this new perspective of separation, the feeling of letting go of control, or losing control, feels like a threat.

But our soul always knows better. Our soul always remembers. Our heart yearns to be open and loving. The desire for freedom and peace always burns within us. But when the ego insists on control, we experience a conflict. Traditionally alcohol, drugs and other forms of behavior that are ultimately destructive have been used to overshadow this conflict.

This is the conflict we find ourselves in. We wish to surrender but the wounded, traumatized child within us is frightened for its survival. It believes that staying in control is the only hope. The free spirit within us remembers the ecstasy and joy of being free. So we understand that our resistance is not a form of weakness, inadequacy or failure, but rather is our will to survive. Our resistance is the amazing ability to adapt.

However as adults, we are in a much different position than we were as children. We are no longer vulnerable and dependent on others for our survival. It's very hard to let go of this idea. The culture supports it. We are reminded constantly that the world is a real power and there are people and events that have real power over us - that we are potential victims in all kinds of circumstances. And this is our dilemma: to remember that the world has no power. We are called to remember that there is actually nothing outside of us and that all that rises into consciousness rises from within us. We are the only threat to our survival. We have the ability to create from infinite potential. We have the ability to create from unlimited possibility. We are victims of nothing. We are powerful creators.

Until now, most of our creative activity has been on an unconscious level. Now, we are recognizing that we can consciously choose to create a very different experience. Now we begin to recognize that there is no threat to our survival from any power outside of us. Now we realize it is safe for us to surrender our control, our hyper-vigilance, our fear. Now we can allow ourselves to be free.

51. DO YOU DESERVE TO FEEL PEACE?

Do you believe that you deserve to feel peace in your life? Is it okay for you to exist without justifying yourself? Is it okay for you to just be here, just as you are? Do you feel pressure to be some way, to accomplish something or to get something done? Do you think it is perfectly fine that you are who you are? Or do you believe that there is a part of you that isn't good enough?

Our spiritual journey teaches us that we are perfect, whole, and complete in this moment. There are absolutely no exceptions. As we become conscious and awake, we see how we have disliked and disapproved of ourselves: how we have judged and condemned ourselves, how we have found ourselves wanting and needing improvement, how we have developed strategies to justify and make ourselves look good so we can avoid the sense that there is basically something wrong or bad about us. There is nothing that so powerfully distracts us from knowing the truth than the inner feeling and belief that there is something wrong with us. We will go to extraordinary lengths to prove that our imperfection is not true - all the while believing it is. If we have to prove that it is not true, we must believe that it is possible for us to be imperfect, and yet our core understanding, our knowledge of the truth, says it is impossible - the truth indicates that there can be no imperfection.

There cannot be something wrong or bad with us, yet we spend time and attention trying to address this point. For many of us the confusion is strong. At some level we believe if we are seen - if we are truly seen - we will be proven bad. So we spend our time making sure that we are not seen. We develop a personality and an identity where we reveal nothing. Vast amounts of energy are consumed to keep that supposedly dark part of us hidden.

Ironically, it isn't the darkness that gets hidden when we try to hide: it is the light. There is no darkness; it only seems dark because we will not look at it. It hurts to open places we have closed. That is why we avoid it. That is why it seems like darkness. And we believe we can control what we perceive as darkness.

We cannot free ourselves and hold those places tightly closed. The authentic part of ourselves is inside the closed places. The love, the vulnerability, the creativity, the connection, is something bigger than us, and these qualities are hidden from us when we won't let ourselves be seen.

When we have to control what others see in us, we have made a judgment – we have condemned ourselves. We have come to believe that this identity is who we are - this creation of our mind that selectively blocks awareness of the truth and is a limited caricature of ourselves. We refuse to accept the truth. We are afraid of what is in us, afraid to give in, afraid to relax.

What would happen if we were free, if we didn't control ourselves, if we didn't go to so much trouble and effort to justify our existence? What if we had the arrogance to believe we have every right to be here - to do whatever we please? What if we didn't have to please anyone? What if we cared nothing about what others thought? What if we did nothing unless we chose to? For many of us that would bring up images of an animal out of control - the worst sort of person.

Certainly those characteristics without benefit of love can be very harsh. We always seem to leave love out of the picture. When we talk about not controlling ourselves we imagine a wild animal. It is hard for us to imagine that letting go of control means freeing our love and light – that it means opening our heart and becoming authentic.

Which context will you choose? One where you are essentially, somehow bad? Will you choose a context that sees you as needing control and discipline – a context where you have to work to justify yourself? Will you decide you won't allow yourself to be seen? Or will you choose the context that sees there is light and the love of God within you? Will you choose a context that knows that is all there is – a context that will increase the peace, joy and love you experience? Or will you continue to beat into shape that part of you which is unacceptable? Can you love and cherish that part of you that is individual and unique, and a perfect expression of God in this moment? Are you going to use effort and force or are you going to open and allow? In this moment can you practice acceptance of who you are, exactly as you are in every way? Can you recognize the presence of God is alive as you? Can you recognize that you are the light?

52. THE PATH OF AWAKENING

What are you doing in this moment? Are you trying to solve a problem? Are you wondering why you can't surrender? Are you wondering why bad things happen to you or why the good things you want don't? If that is what you are doing, stop. You already know the answer to all your questions, but that answer isn't available to your thinking. A thinking mind can only solve problems that have logical answers - mathematical problems, engineering problems, etc. The answers to our real questions lie in the creative and intuitive realm. And in fact in this realm, the questions rapidly become irrelevant.

When we first see the promise of the awakened life - of becoming conscious - when we see what is truly possible, we know this is the path for us. We know at some point we have no choice but to follow this path: the path of awakening, the path of becoming conscious, the path of surrendering and trusting. As we move along the path, we find that certain types of resistance - which we may not be conscious of - keep repeating themselves in our lives as if there is a lesson we cannot learn.

When there is a lesson we can't learn, there is something that remains unconscious. For each of us this is expressed differently. We express resistance uniquely in different aspects of our lives, but the process is always the same. For the truth is that until the ego surrenders, we live in fear of that which we want the most. And although we know we want to surrender, we know we want peace, we know we want abundance, and freedom, our fear matches our desire and blocks our attainment. As long as we have faith in our ego, as long as one of our major concerns is to look good - to control how we are seen - we are at the mercy of the fear of shame, humiliation and annihilation that lies behind that desire.

So we continue to block our own good. This is not an unnatural process. It is not wrong or bad. But it would come to an end much more quickly if we could stop judging. If we moved more quickly to acceptance, if we trusted more easily that what was unfolding was perfect, if we allowed ourselves to more freely express our truth in the moment, if we accepted ourselves in this moment exactly as we are, we would stop blocking our good. There is never any need for judgment or any cause for shame or blame. There is never anything wrong or bad. But the ego will not understand that, and any degree of faith placed in the ego leads to the experience of duality. The more we believe in good and bad, the more we experience it. The more we believe in right and wrong the more we experience it. The more we accept *what is* as perfect, the more we experience perfection. It seems too simple, but it is that simple.

In this moment, you could surrender. You could experience the light and love, the peace, the oneness, the unity, the joy, and the bliss that is alive right now - that is the truth right now. If that is not what you are experiencing, what are you experiencing?

You are experiencing resistance. What are you doing with that experience? Are you judging it? Are you frustrated, tired? Can you feel the fear that underlies the resistance? Can you become conscious of your own determination to not surrender? Can you be conscious of your own *no*? Can you love that *no*? Can you accept it?

Resistance does not arise from the conscious level of the mind; it arises from what is unconscious. In the end, what you are unconscious of is fear. You are afraid to surrender, to give in, to let go, and to give up control. Are you aware of that fear? It is only natural that you would have it. It is not a cause for shame and judgment. It is not a reason for you to feel inadequate, unworthy or broken. It is simply a natural response that over time has become deeply buried in the unconscious. If you cannot feel it, there is no cause for alarm. We know that it's there by the simple fact that we can't surrender. And so we see that there is something we long for. We long for surrender - release of tension and holding. We long for the peace of knowing we are whole and complete. We long for the joy of spontaneous expression. We long for freedom from fear.

So we practice allowing and accepting. We experience our resistance. We understand that there is fear and our task in this moment is to bring the light and love to the darkness and fear by allowing an attitude of acceptance, gratitude, compassion, and understanding. This means we don't judge and we accept unconditionally everything that is real in this moment; we stop analyzing, evaluating, judging and we just experience. There is nothing to be done. There is only allowing what already is, to be. We can only do that when we stop.

53. IT'S COMPLETELY YOUR CHOICE

How do you feel about yourself in this moment? What kind of opinions and judgments are you holding? What kind of thoughts are passing through your mind about who you are or what you are doing? Are there ways in which you are holding back from feeling good? Are there ways you're not allowing yourself to feel joy, peace, or love? Is there something you feel needs to change before you can allow yourself to be okay? Are you waiting to improve something, or to achieve some kind of level of development before you can really feel good about yourself? Do you have goals and standards to meet before you can believe that you are fine the way you are? How many ways do you fall short of where you think you should be? How many times a day do you think, *I should be doing something differently or better or, there must be something wrong with me?*

Right now, right in this moment, can you allow yourself to feel good? Can you allow yourself just to say, *I am fine, I will be fine, everything is fine*? What happens when you think that? Can you allow yourself to say, *All is well, all is perfect, I can relax now, there is no pressure, I am not in danger, and there is no threat to my survival*? Do you hear internal objections or arguments? Do you feel fear or resistance? Or are you enjoying the peace of letting go and becoming quiet and still?

For so many of us, happiness is something to be earned. It is not something we expect to feel just any time. We have become accustomed to the idea that it's going to be hard to be happy. There's so much to do. We think we have to perform. We have to be good. We have to do what we're supposed to do or we deserve the bad things that come to us for not being good enough. The endless treadmill of the ego continues but we do not have to be part of it. We don't have to believe it. We don't have to believe in it.

We already know there is a truth that is present in every moment. That truth never changes. In truth we are already perfect. We cannot be anything else. We know that truth cannot judge, criticize, or measure. It can only be what it already is, what it always has been and what it always will be. We know that truth is present within us as a living, vital force - the life force - the very energy that gives us life. Every particle of our being is made from this stuff – this love in form. We know this is true, but we are more comfortable trusting our ego and what we make up with our mind. We prefer to believe what we see with our eyes and what we hear with our ears. We are far more comfortable with ideas of lack, hardship, struggle and suffering. We cannot bear the idea of looking bad, making a mistake, or failing. This is what is really important to us, even though we know what the ego says is a dream and an illusion. There is no power in this illusion, no satisfaction, no joy, no life in it. But it's what we're used to. And it is not nearly as frightening as peace, joy and love expressed spontaneously. It is not nearly as frightening as opening our hearts and loving unconditionally, or as taking full responsibility for our world and what happens in it, or as frightening as creating powerfully, living in beauty and richness, peace, joy, tranquility, love, bliss. None of the promised benefits can lure us away from the comfort of controlling our world.

Right now, in this moment, the doorway is open to all we want. All you can imagine or dream is available to you right now. You don't have to do anything to earn it or to achieve it. You simply need to give up the addiction to being comfortable. Are you willing to take the risk of losing your comfort for the opportunity to gain everything? This is not a scam. This is not a con or a marketing trick. This is the truth taught by the wisest spiritual teachers of humanity. This is your birthright. This is your true nature. We are not talking about an act of will to create into some new form. Instead we are talking about allowing what is already true to become conscious, to be your experience - to fill your awareness and replace the dreams of comfort and safety that come with controlling your life experience. All the power, love, and energy of the universe – the energy that creates the universe - are in you right now. There is no distance between you and anything. There is no separation between you and anything. There is no you but the you that is the mind of the universe. The world is not your master. You are not a slave or a victim.

You are a creator whether you choose to create from the comfort and safety of controlling yourself or you choose to create from the spontaneous, joyful awareness of the power that is available to you. It's completely your choice. Whether you persist in creating a life of joy and peace or insist on hardship, struggle, and judgment is totally your choice. You are never a victim. You may not be aware that you are choosing, but you are. And so in this moment, as in every single moment, you can choose to trust and surrender, to accept the perfection that is the only possibility of reality, or you can choose to dream of falling short, of controlling, and of failing. Reality or dream: one brings peace, the other brings stress.

If you hear or feel the words, *I can't surrender, I can't let go, I can't get there,* you are listening to the ego and you are taking the role of a victim. Rather say, *I won't let go, I won't surrender, I am afraid.* And then say, *But I know that it is perfect, I know it cannot be any other way in this moment, I know it means nothing about me, because there cannot be anything but perfection. My inability to feel completely surrendered is perfect. I accept it. I will not fight it. I say 'yes' to my fear, to my need to control. I know how important these have been to me in ways that I cannot see at the moment. It is all perfect. I remember that God is at work here and there is only perfection. I remember that my mind cannot comprehend the full picture, but that is no reason for me to hold back and to not trust, not let go, not accept my own perfection - my own divine nature. My divine nature is the only reality. All else is a dream.*

54. YOUR TASK IN THIS MOMENT

Consider this: there is nothing in this moment to which you are a victim. There is nothing controlling you, nothing blocking you, nothing doing anything to you. Everything you experience in this moment is a direct result of choices you are making right now, either consciously or unconsciously.

This is not to say that your experience should be different. This idea is not a judgment of your experience in this moment; it does not mean it is somehow flawed. It is said to bring into your awareness the knowledge of your own power to choose your experience. Some of the choices you are making in this moment may be so deeply unconscious that you cannot conceive of them as a choice. This is the journey of expansion and evolution, the journey of becoming conscious.

There is one certainty in this moment: you can choose where to place your attention. You may be distracted easily; it may feel like effort or struggle. But you can choose. And every time you choose, your focus grows stronger. You can choose in this moment to fill your mind with thoughts of the truth - to align yourself with what you know to be true. You can choose to prepare your mind to become open and accepting, still and silent, and be under your direction.

To bring to mind in this moment our knowledge of the truth, we remind ourselves that there is only one power right now - there is nothing against us but our own choices. That power is present and alive in every particle of this physical universe right now. It is infinite and eternal. Nothing can corrupt it, diminish it or taint it in any way. It is timeless and formless, invisible, but present. It doesn't matter what we feel or think. It is always true. It is always the only thing there is. There is no objection, no argument, and no case against it. We cannot make it go away. We cannot shut it down. It does not withhold or judge.

It – this power - is creating everything about you in this moment. There is nothing about you that is not it. Yes, you are unique. You are an individual, but you are not separate. This is the truth we dwell on: we train our mind in this moment to pay attention to nothing but this truth. We make the choice to accept it as true.

Because we accept and acknowledge this truth, we know right now we are safe. There is no threat to our survival. There is no threat to our existence. There is no danger in this moment. It is only life - the loving creative power of God expressing as the life force in us and as us right now. This is real power. There is nothing blocking you right now except your choice. It is your choice right now to accept and live in the truth - to pay attention only to the truth. Even when your experience is uncomfortable or painful you have the choice to dwell in the truth.

You may have an expectation of what you should experience. You may have an expectation of what you should feel or how you should be. If you let go of that and become present to *what is* in this moment – if you dwell on the truth that is always true in this moment and accept the expression of life exactly as it is in this moment - your experience will change. There is no way that you *should* be. There is nothing that you *should* experience.

Life is unfolding. Life is expanding and evolving. There is no end-point. There is an expansion of consciousness, waking up, of becoming more and more deeply aware of the presence and the power of God within you. This begins with focusing your mind on the truth.

There is nothing wrong with you. You are not failing. You are not broken. You are not inadequate. You are pure spirit in form. You have created your own limitations, struggles and challenges. That is to be expected. It is the natural order. None of it changes the truth in any way. None of your life denies your perfection in any way.

Your task in this moment isn't to make yourself better - to bring yourself to some standard. Your task is to simply accept the undeniable, natural perfection and harmony that is your life no matter how it looks or feels. The basis of all your suffering is your non-acceptance. Nothing else causes suffering. There is no power against you and no control over you. Nothing is missing or broken. It is only your insistence that something is wrong that makes it wrong. In this moment, life is flowing perfectly. Divine light and love are present in every particle, every cell, every molecule - every aspect of your being. There is only one thing that is real in this moment and that is the presence and the power of God. If you choose to become quiet and still, you will experience this truth. You will be filled with the light.

55. FEAR OF LIFE WITHIN US

Are you aware that you act, think and believe you are all alone and have to solve every problem by yourself? Do you believe there are limitations that you can't seem to overcome? Do you think you are not where you should be? Perhaps you should be healthier, wealthier, more beautiful, smarter, more expressive, more connected, more grounded, more flexible? How big is your list of areas where you fall short of your expectations of where you should be? Note carefully this important point: there is a big difference between feeling you should be something and you wanting to be something. Wanting to be healthier, stronger, or wealthier is different than feeling that you *should* be any of those and that you are not getting there.

Many of us walk around with lists of ways our life is not good enough - ways we fall short. We feel disappointed, frustrated, ashamed, and embarrassed because as hard as we try, we don't know how to change any of it. We have forgotten that we can access infinite intelligence, infinite wisdom, the source of all creation – we can access miracles. We have forgotten that the part of us that believes in limitation – the part that believes we are alone and that we must do it ourselves - is not who we are.

We believe that we are disconnected from reality. What we're living seems like reality - it is the reality we grew up with so we don't challenge it. We go along with it.

More and more we will remember that the source of our pain, discomfort and frustration. It is our belief system, our identity, our ego - our story. There is nothing else causing us pain or suffering – nothing else at all. It is our insistence that something is wrong, that something should be different, that somehow this moment is not perfect, that causes pain. And why do we fall into this trap? Because we are afraid; we are afraid of the life within us. We are afraid of the power within us. We were led to believe that we are destructive and that we could destroy relationships. We came to believe in our power to hurt. We fear we might do something that would make us undesirable. Our ego holds the view that something within us must be kept under control at all times – we must not let that part of us ever be seen or expressed. And so we have rules of behavior.

What we are not conscious of is that we sacrifice our health, our freedom, and our access to abundance and creativity in the name of what seems like safety, what seems like being good, what seems like being a decent person. As if we were really something else. We fear we are not a decent or good person. Maybe we are hateful or have murderous rage, or maybe we are pathetic. This is our fear. This is why we go along with the ego and the identity and this is why we end up feeling alone and powerless to change anything. What we really want to do is make ourselves into a better person so we don't have to confront that ugly side. We want to become pure like saints. And we believe we can do it with hard work and will power.

Have we ever considered that there is a part of us that we are so afraid of that we will give up much to keep that part hidden? And that that part of us is actually - simply - a living, dynamic expression of spirit and nothing more? Have we considered that what we see and are so afraid of is the spontaneous expression of the life force – a force that exists without judgment? This life force is a powerful energy that seeks expression and never stops seeking expression. Just like water running downhill, it does not stop when it runs into a rock. It builds up until it goes around or over the rock and continues to run downhill. And so the life force within us continues to express in the face of any obstacle. This is what our ego cannot tolerate. This is what our identity was designed to protect us against.

So we sit right here, right now, and we long for the experience of peace and surrender but only in ways that are acceptable to the ego. Our intention to surrender is conditional. We are not willing to surrender to whatever; we are only willing to surrender to what the ego determines as good. We are not interested in surrendering to grief, hate, sorrow, rage, hopelessness or despair – all of which would be a natural reaction, an authentic response. *Do not misunderstand these words.* There is no implication that anything is wrong or bad. These words are only about seeking consciousness - of bringing light to that which we have not seen. We may be choosing to believe in something that is imagined and not something that is real: separation, lack of power, lack of intelligence, lack of wisdom, lack of any kind. But it can only be imaginary as these qualities are not real.

All that we yearn for is good, and is available, present and real right now. No matter what we are paying attention to in this moment, reality remains the same. A perfect, loving, divine, creative power is giving us life in this moment. We are expressing that power perfectly in this moment. We are exercising the gift of choice and imagination in this moment.

56. THE EGO'S ROLE

In a previous discussion we spoke of how the ego could be likened to a life-long friend with whom we had become very comfortable. Perhaps you have had a friend in your life, who speaks with such authority and confidence that you believed what they said even if it went against your intuition. This is exactly the way we relate to the ego. Our intuition or emotional guidance system says, *I want this* or, *I don't want this*, and the ego says, *you have to, you should, it is better.* And we listen. But who is listening to the ego? Who is going along with it?

We are not used to the idea that we are not the ego. The voice has been in our head so long we don't know that it is not us. It is important to discern this voice, recognize it for what it is, and realize that there is someone listening to the ego that is much closer to who we are than the ego.

As humans, we have the unique ability to recognize ourselves as *I.* We are able to distinguish our individual expressions of spirit, and consciously differentiate ourselves from the environment around us. That ability is a two-edged sword. It has led us to believe the stories of the ego – stories such as, we are separate, and that there is something special about us – a specialness that can be expressed as lack, grandiosity, narcissism, or victimization.

The ego's role is to make us different. The truth is that being aware of ourselves does not mean we are separate. It means we have limited our self-awareness to what we *think*. We are perfectly capable of being aware of our limited self. That is what intuition and guidance are - the awareness of more than just our ego self. So we see that in a sense, we have chosen the ego as our guide, as our best friend, as the authority in our lives, as the diviner of what is good and bad and right and wrong, as the authority for what will work and what won't work, and the guide for how to be. We want to become aware of both that we are making this choice, and when we are making it so we can choose to make another choice.

We know there is something more to us than what our ego presents. We long for the peace and freedom that we know is possible. But the only way the ego knows how to make change is to manipulate the physical world. The ego is a product of the physical world. It knows nothing about the invisible. When we long for change, the ego tells us to change or pay attention to something in the physical world. It tells us to fight, to work hard, to accomplish, to do, or to make things happen. This is a compelling argument. It can work for a short time, but if followed, all we have achieved is strengthening the ego's ideas.

There are times when the issues in the physical world are so intrusive that they must be resolved before we can shift our attention and our awareness to the non-physical. But in reality this is not the case most of the time. In reality, most of what seems to be the physical world intruding is the ego creating distractions. So right now, in this moment, the invisible world is present, alive, and real. And we will become aware of it if we stop listening to the ego - to the mind. We will become aware of the invisible if we stop trying to change things and leave behind the idea of doing something to make us better - if we take this moment just as it is and leave behind the idea of changing anything except what we are paying attention to. We have come to trust our ego so completely that we fear the idea of it becoming quiet. Our faith is in our ego. This is what we trust.

Now it's time to place our faith in what we know is the truth. Now is the time to place our faith in the one power, spirit, the universal energy of life.

Become still. Become quiet. Listen to what is present in this moment. Feel this moment. Become aware of all there is to perceive in this moment. You can trust. You are safe. You are a child of God. All the power of God is alive within you right now - all of it. All the love of God is alive as you. It is not out of reach; it is not illusive; it is not a secret. It is the truth of who you are. It has not denied you. It has not been withheld from you. It is real right now. Do not concern yourself with resistance. Just allow yourself to be.

57. WANTING AN IMPROVED LIFE

There is much talk, discussion and teaching about how to get what you want, how to become connected, how to be a good person, how to become real. There is a bewildering array of techniques, schools of thought, spiritual teachers and channels - all of which contain some element of truth. These truths catch our interest. It can be hard to understand what is wrong when we don't get the results promised by teacher after teacher, technique after technique. It is difficult to understand why things look essentially the same despite our efforts.

Of course we are all experiencing some kind of growth and expansion – it is inevitable. But we may feel there are certain areas in our life that keep repeating the same things over and over, no matter how much help we get. In these teachings, much attention is given to the physical world. We are directed to make life-changes, improvements in career, enhance our health and wealth, manifest desires, and live our dreams. The outward appearance becomes the measure of our spiritual practice and development. It is implied that if we aren't able to manifest a new car or a significant monthly income, we are not spiritually developed. The truth is - as painful as it may be to hear for people experiencing difficulties - manipulating the physical world is trivial compared to the journey of surrendering the ego completely.

This surrender is the only journey that has worthwhile results. Tinkering and manipulating the physical world is fun, it feels good and it brings rewards, but the hunger for authenticity does not go away. The hunger for love, for true connection and knowledge is always knocking at the door. We know the ego is at work when we feel there is something we need, there is something missing, something we want. What we truly, deeply, and authentically want is to be ourselves to the fullest degree -to have no limitations, no fetters, no chains. It is easy to think that more money, more health, or a nicer house will bring this about, but of course it won't. It won't because we are looking in the wrong direction. As soon as we feel we need or want anything we are disconnected from truth - when we are connected, everything is already present. When we are focused on the truth, and being exactly who we are, we are love. Our desire is to give not to get. Our desire is to be not to do, to express to the fullest degree possible the beauty and wonder of life.

We have no need to draw things to us. We have a need to express the fullness, the completeness, the wholeness, the infinite vastness of who we are. All the great teachers explain that the entire universe exists within us. There is nothing we lack; there is nothing missing. That has not changed. That will never change. We cannot look to the world for answers. Our journey is to find ourselves. Our task is to learn to make the steps back to what is truly real, truly authentic. When we cling tightly to the limitations that seem to protect us, when there is great fear and pain around letting go, becoming conscious, waking up, and releasing the past, it is not always an easy and comfortable journey.

In one way we are becoming less, not more; we already are everything and to that we add our ideas of limitation. What your mind says and your ego says is of no relevance. The truth is the truth. It always will be, it always has been, and it is right now. Whether your mind and ego go along with that is of no consequence. They are not a power, they are not the truth, and they are not the source of reality. They are a distraction we have chosen to become addicted to.

Giving up addictions is difficult and painful. It takes commitment and courage. Not one of us would like to admit how glad we are of our resistance - the ways in which we are able to be distracted. We have poor health, we don't have a job, we don't have money, we don't have this or that. Focusing on our victimization is much easier than letting go.

So in this moment we face the choice: is this moment perfect or not? Are we perfect or not? It doesn't mean there is anything wrong if your ego screams objections to the idea that this moment is perfect or you are perfect. If a list of imperfections starts to roll through your mind, it means you are paying attention to your mind or your ego. That is where you place your faith. And there is nothing wrong with that. We will not change something until we are conscious of it. The truth is, we know for a fact this moment is perfect and we are perfect. Whether we choose to pay attention to this truth or the ego makes no difference. It doesn't change the truth. Truth continues to be true whether we pay attention to it or not. Watching and believing in the movie of our identity and ego does not change anything. Truth cannot be changed. And so, in this moment we face the choice: *Will I align with the truth or my identity?*

58. STOP THE FIGHT

It is useful, from time to time, to consider the concept of surrender, what we mean by it and why we use that term. In general, the meaning of surrender is to let go of something, to give in to something. Both meanings imply that we are actively holding on to something or opposing something. Surrender implies that we can stop doing something. So if we are going to surrender, it may be useful to understand what we are surrendering. What is it that we are holding on to or we are opposing that we want to stop? It seems both meanings are useful when we come to meditation for what we are holding onto are belief systems, ideas, and identity. And what are we opposing, what are we fighting against, what are we afraid to give in to, to allow to overtake us? We are fighting and opposing our very core nature from overtaking us from our most authentic feelings and energy. We are opposing the truth. Control is probably what we grip the tightest. We are controlling what we express so that it fits with our identity and our beliefs. This controlling and opposing is not simply an abstract mental process. It is happening on the physical level.

We are gripping tightly with our bodies to prevent the free-flow of energy, to control our outward expression.

There was a time when the free expression of our authentic self appeared to be a threat to our survival. At great cost and great pain we began to control it. That grip on ourselves became hardened until it was so unconscious that we don't even notice it. But the pulsation and flow of life within us never ceases until we die. It pushes against our resistance – always. It's always seeking expansion and free expression – greater and greater expression. This causes great conflict within us, perhaps mostly at an unconscious level, but we see its effect in our lives. We see the health issues, the physical discomfort, deterioration of our physical fitness, headaches, stomach problems, feet problems, knees and hips, shoulders and neck. All because we are afraid of what lies within us – what we will look like if we express ourselves freely, what will happen to our relationships and our place in the world if we are not controlled and presentable.

To surrender, we must relax our grip. We must begin to let go of the holding and the controlling. We must let that which is authentic and real flow freely once again. There is another form of control where surrender is needed; that is our faith in our mind and ego – our belief that we are all alone and that we must do everything on our own, that our answer lies with our ego, and in finding out what is right and wrong, good or bad. We must surrender to a greater intelligence. We must surrender to the truth of one power. We must let go of the idea of separation. We must let go of duality, of judgment and commit our faith to the one power, to align ourselves in this moment with the knowledge that perfection is the only reality. We are fully capable of dreaming imperfection, pretending it is real, but it never can be, never will be. It is only our insistence that makes it seem as if it could be real. We are standing in the kingdom of heaven with our eyes closed and our hands over our ears shouting, *it's not real. Hell is real. Heaven is not real.*

Now is the moment to surrender that fight, surrender that control, give in now, allow the ego to lose the battle. Surrender is the victory. Surrender is the evidence of courage. Surrender brings the prize. Surrender is a conscious choice, the conscious aligning and accepting of the truth, accepting the perfection of this moment. Beyond all doubt it is perfect. Give in now, stop the fight, stop the effort, stop the control. Stop screaming *this is hell* and open your inner vision and look at heaven around you. The truth is that love flows through you, fills every particle of your being, brings life to every cell of your body as an alive and real presence within you right now. It is even more real than your body.

ABOUT THE AUTHORS

Michael and Judy currently live on the island of Maui in Hawaii. They have committed themselves to expansion of their awareness and consciousness so they may be free in their expression of who they truly are – which they do for the most part through music, dancing, and helping others to do the same.

Visit www.openingandallowing.com to find out more about the intuitive source of this book. You can find out more about Judy and her work as an intuitive guide at www.judy-flores.com. To find out more about Michael and his music and recorded meditations, visit www.michaelwarmuth.com.

THE SOURCE OF THESE MEDITATIONS

In 2008, during a period of significant life changes, Michael committed himself more deeply to a path of surrender and allowing his authentic self to be revealed. As a result of this commitment he explored many avenues of spiritual growth and development and his spiritual practice became the main focus for his life. Through a series of events during this time, what might be called a channel was opened in Michael's consciousness. This channel now enables him to access a source of wisdom and knowledge that was not previously available to him, and would not normally be a part of our conscious awareness. It is tempting to see this source as a separate being or entity, but through questioning Michael and Judy were able to determine that this source is actually a universal consciousness, potentially available to everyone. The information and guidance from this source has been an important guide for Michael and Judy.

Since 2011, Michael has been using this source to lead a guided meditation every morning, which is recorded and then transcribed by Judy. The meditations in this book all have this origin.

Made in the USA
Charleston, SC
04 August 2016